THE LAWYERS FIELD GUIDE TO EFFECTIVE BUSINESS DEVELOPMENT

WILLIAM J. FLANNERY, JR.

LawPractice Management Section
MARKETING • MANAGEMENT • TECHNOLOGY • FINANCE

Nothing contained in this book is to be considered as the rendering of legal advice for specific cases, and readers are responsible for obtaining such advice from their own legal counsel. This book and any forms and agreements herein are intended for educational and informational purposes only.

Cover design by ABA Publishing.

The Law Practice Management Section of the American Bar Association offers an educational program for lawyers in practice. Books and other materials are published in furtherance of that program. Authors and editors of publications may express their own legal interpretations and opinions, which are not necessarily those of either the American Bar Association or the Law Practice Management Section unless adopted pursuant to the bylaws of the Association. The opinions expressed do not reflect in any way a position of the Section or the American Bar Association, nor do the positions of the Section or the American Bar Association necessarily reflect the opinions of the author.

The products and services mentioned in this publication are under trademark or service-mark protection. Product and service names and terms are used throughout only in an editorial fashion, to the benefit of the product manufacturer or service provider, with no intention of infringement. Use of a product or service name or term in this publication should not be regarded as affecting the validity of any trademark or service mark.

Library of Congress Cataloging-in-Publication Data

The Lawyer's Field Guide to Effective Business Development. Flannery, William J., Jr.: Library of Congress Cataloging-in-Publication Data is on file.

ISBN-13: 978-1-59031-736-5
ISBN-10: 1-59031-736-X

10 09   5 4 3

Discounts are available for books ordered in bulk. Special consideration is given to state bars, CLE programs, and other bar-related organizations. Inquire at Book Publishing, American Bar Association, 321 N. Clark Street, Chicago, Illinois 60610.

Table of Contents

About the Author

William J. Flannery, Jr., J.D.
President, The WJF Institute

Bill Flannery is the President of The WJF Institute, headquartered in Austin, Texas. The Institute's primary focus is business development, client development, client relationship management, law firm marketing, and marketing support programs. From 1988 to 2006, The WJF Institute has conducted intensive, small-group training sessions for over 10,000 lawyers all over the world.

Bill graduated from the University of Maryland at College Park, MD in 1967. He started his career in 1966 at the Department of Justice as an instructor. He later joined the Johns-Manville Corporation in their Washington, DC, office. In 1969, he joined the IBM Corporation in Washington, DC. While at IBM, he attended the University of Baltimore Law School and obtained his Juris Doctorate in 1973. He also attended the IBM/Harvard Advanced Business Executive Education Institute.

His IBM career included assignments in marketing training, product marketing, large account marketing, IBM corporate executive briefing program, corporate strategic planning, finance, litigation management, personal computer product development, and technology for the legal profession.

He was instrumental in creating a new IBM marketing group specializing in technology systems for the legal profession: The IBM Legal Profession Marketing Group (LPM). The IBM

LPM Group was created in January 1980 in response to the growing technology systems needs of the private practice, courts, governments, and in-house counsel here in the U.S. and overseas. As a member of IBM's LPM Group, his responsibilities included IBM's relationships with key law firm computer customers, corporate law departments' in-house legal systems managers, and IBM's outside counsel. He left IBM in 1988 and founded The WJF Institute.

Bill has been a special advisor to the ABA and the Association of Legal Administrators (ALA) on technology and marketing. He has served as a member of the ALA's Long Range Planning Committee. He has lectured on strategic planning, technology and business development, sales, and marketing at law schools as well as graduate and undergraduate schools in the U.S. and overseas.

Bill has published numerous articles on business development, marketing, technology, and law firm management in law journals and legal publications. He is a frequent speaker at Legal Marketing Association and other legal conferences.

The WJF Institute's Client Development and Relationship Management workshop was selected as a semifinalist in Inc. magazine's Marketing Masters Awards in 1997 for innovative marketing programs. Bill and the instructor staff at The WJF Institute have extensive experience in sales, marketing consulting, and training with various companies in The Fortune 500, The Global 1000, international brokerage firms, international accounting firms, high-tech companies, information services companies, world-wide court reporting firms, litigation support providers, software companies, financial institutions and a broad range of sophisticated consulting firms whose clients are the Fortune 500 and Global 1000.

Acknowledgments

My deepest gratitude and professional admiration to:

— Bruce Tucker, for his incredible creative writing suggestions.

— Beverly Loder and Deborah McMurray, for their insights and guidance.

My sincerest thanks to:

— Peggy Dieterich and Susan Sosa, my indispensable assistants.

— Current and past WJF Institute instructors: Jana Ames, Ginna Bekassy, David Braun, Alan Ceshker, Barbara Clay, Sheryl Draker, Linda Fleming, Dale Head, Trey Herschap, Iris Jones, Michael Kerrs, Chris Kirby, Logan Loomis, Wayne Lovett, Nancy Mangan, Kevin McMurdo, Joel Momberger, Mark Murdock, Sona Pancholy, Rob Randolph, David Reiter, Shelby Rogers, Sharon Schweitzer, Keith Shuley, Cathy Tabor, Linda Truxell, Bill Wilson, Loren Wittner.

— Catherine Austin, Steve Boutwell, Ed Burke, Kipley Bruketa, Logan Chandler, Bill Cobb, Ron Cullis, Suzanne Donnels, Tim Durkin, Ross Fishman, Gary Garrett, Ann Lee Gibson, Jeanne Hammerstrom, Richard Levick, Paul Lisnek, Logan Loomis, Laura Meherg, Barbara Miller, Bill Nardiello, Jolene Overbeck, Jennifer Phillips, Pike Powers, Jane Sullivan Roberts, Ron Shapiro, Ann Wallace, Mary Weber, Peter Zeughauser.

— Our many clients, all over the world.

My love to:

—My mother, Dorothy Sheftall Flannery, my father, William Jackson Flannery, Tobie, Kevin, Billy, Melita, Will, Madeline, Max and Molly.

Foreword

Bill Flannery and I first met near the time that he founded The WJF Institute to teach lawyers how to build client relationships. Since that time, I have attended his seminars and hired him to train other lawyers. We have also spent extensive informal time together talking about the principles, strategies, and tactics that he has developed and taught to others over the years. So, I know a fair amount about the substance of his thinking, and I can tell you that this Field Guide is a near-perfect distillation of Bill's wisdom on the topic of business development for lawyers.

I say "wisdom" because Bill has spent years refining his ideas and testing them against the realities of business development in the unique environment of legal practice. And I say "near-perfect" because no book can really capture the excitement of Bill Flannery's enthusiastic, animated presentation style. But as compensation for missing the experience of watching Bill in action, you have in this Field Guide a ready reference that you can keep and use repeatedly in your own business development activities. I have enjoyed reading it, and plan to keep it close by for further reference. I wish the same for each of you.

Rick Salwen
Former General Counsel, Dell, Inc.

Preface

When the Law Practice Management Section of the ABA selected me to write a book on business development for lawyers, I immediately did three things:

1. I surveyed the marketing and business development professionals in law firms;

2. I reviewed the existing ABA publications on marketing and business development; and

3. I surveyed the clients of The WJF Institute.

The results of these surveys and subsequent analysis led me to conclude that what's missing in the business development literature and what many lawyers sorely need is a practical guide to acquiring and refining the face-to-face skills necessary for winning and keeping profitable clients. Hence this Field Guide.

A focus on face-to-face skills and tactics in business development has been the foundation of the WJF Institute's work since 1989. During that time, we have helped more than 10,000 lawyers—from solo practitioners, small firms, medium firms, large international firms, government entities, and corporate law departments—master the art and science of creating, developing, maintaining, and growing their "book of business." This Field Guide is intended to bring to an even wider audience those proven methods of business development and put their power right in your hands.

Marketing, business development, and sales have been a way of life for me since 1963. This book reflects that experience as well as the wisdom of those who have influenced my thinking and work. To those who have in ways large and small helped shape the ideas and methods that appear here I offer a heartfelt thank you. To those about to encounter those ideas and methods in the pages that follow I can assure you that they can work for you.

Introduction:
Why a "Field Guide"?

Long-term, profitable client relationships form the foundation for the enduring success of any law firm. In addition to quantifiable economic benefits, such relationships generate numerous other business benefits such as higher morale and lower turnover, and the increased ability to recruit talented associates eager to work with attractive clients and do exciting legal work. Although less easily quantified, those benefits, too, ultimately contribute to profitability.

Such client relationships also enable lawyers to exercise their skills in more significant and rewarding contexts, to experience the satisfaction that comes from serving clients really well, and to have the kind of personal and professional experiences that drew them to a legal career in the first place.

Winning and retaining long-term, attractive clients doesn't happen by accident. No matter how sophisticated your firm's marketing or its client relationship management technology, client relationships almost invariably begin—or never get off the ground—as the result of individual encounters between a lawyer and a prospect. Managing those encounters and maintaining the relationships that grow out of them requires passion, energy, discipline, focus, and highly specific skills. To successfully build and manage a profitable book of business you must be able to:

■ engender trust with prospective clients from the very first meeting;

■ master interpersonal communications skills that enable you to take those first meetings beyond rapport to genuine trust;

■ follow a step-by-step, repeatable process that results in long-term, profitable client relationships;

■ establish financial and qualitative measurements to determine at any point in a client relationship the profitability as well as the non-financial rewards associated with the relationship;

■ provide quality legal services and meet clients' needs in an extraordinary manner; and

■ maintain a balance among the competing claims of legal work, business development, and life outside of work.

Unfortunately, those skills aren't taught in law school and few law firms offer such training. It's not surprising then that many lawyers, faced with the necessity of building business, often find it an onerous task or even try to evade it insofar as possible. People are rarely comfortable attempting complex tasks for which they feel unprepared, especially tasks that depend on their personal qualities. This Field Guide is designed to reduce that discomfort. It lays out a clear sequence of action steps that practitioners can follow to master the skills of business development and, incidentally, to acquire the confidence to use those skills over and over to turn what was once a source of anxiety into a resounding triumph.

Who Should Read This Guide

All lawyers, regardless of their practice, their clients, the type of law firm, the geographic location, or the size of the firm can benefit from the principles and techniques provided here. That includes in-house lawyers in all types of organizations: corporations, medical, educational and government institutions, non-profit organizations, and charities. And, yes, it even includes sports and entertainment lawyers, who may already be outgoing but nevertheless lack some of the basic business development skills that could harness the full power of their gregariousness. The law firm's professional staff should also read this guide in order to understand how they can best support the firm's business development efforts.

How to Use This Guide

The chapters are organized chronologically to take you step by step from your initial search for profitable clients all the way through the process of building and maintaining long-term profitable client relationships (see Figure 1).

This proven, five-step process enables you to:

■ repeat success and avoid unintended outcomes;

■ focus on client needs;

■ obtain measurable results;

■ create a new, more positive mind-set about business development;

■ adopt a firm-wide approach; and

■ clearly establish roles for everyone in the firm.

Figure 1. The Client Development and Relationship Management Process

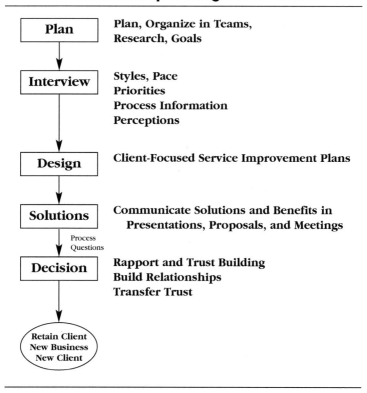

Plan	**Plan, Organize in Teams, Research, Goals**
Interview	**Styles, Pace Priorities Process Information Perceptions**
Design	**Client-Focused Service Improvement Plans**
Solutions	**Communicate Solutions and Benefits in Presentations, Proposals, and Meetings**
Process Questions	
Decision	**Rapport and Trust Building Build Relationships Transfer Trust**
Retain Client New Business New Client	

In order to help you stay oriented as you read, the particular step under discussion appears in the right-hand margin of each right-hand page.

We have also included a number of other helpful features, designed to enable you to access quickly and conveniently the information you need to fully understand the concepts presented here.

Glossary of Terms: These definitions of the terms that you will encounter as you move through the five-step business development process are intended to make clear precisely what is under discussion. Because my experience with glossaries tells me that as readers we rarely look up words at the back of the book, I have put the glossary up front. Readers can gain a full understanding of business development terminology *before* they embark on the heart of the book.

 Gems: Where an idea, concept, action step, or important insight might be found, we have placed this symbol, a gem, to identify these helpful tips.

> **Rule:** Near the end of each chapter, in a shaded box like this one, we have provided a rule that encapsulates the thrust of the chapter.

Appendix A: This offers the most effective way to pursue the five-step business development process for firms of differing sizes and types, including

- solo practitioners;

- small law firms (2 to 25 lawyers);

- medium-sized law firms (25 to 100 lawyers);

- large law firms (100+ lawyers);

- government lawyers; and

- corporate law departments.

Appendix B: An article entitled "Opinion Surveys Can Help Keep Clients Happy" provides a deeper look at one of the most effective tools of business development.

Appendix C: Gems and Rules: The gems and rules, in the order in which they appear in the book, are gathered here for easy review.

Bibliography: This list of additional resources has been organized by mapping them against the various steps in the business development process. Books, articles, or Internet resources that do not clearly fall within a given step in the business development process have been listed in alphabetical order.

These features are designed to equip you with everything you need to engage immediately in more effective business development. Use them. Not just as aids to better understanding, but as indispensable tools that you take with you as you seek to build business. Remember, this is a field guide. Carry it in the glove compartment, in your briefcase, on the airplane. Refer to it often, especially right before you are about to encounter a prospect. Scan the gems. Review the summary of rules. Revisit what's most effective for your kind of firm. And dislodge from your thinking, as often as necessary, the crippling myths that keep you from achieving the breakthrough results that await.

Glossary of Terms

Business Development: All of those activities associated with getting in front of clients or prospective clients face-to-face and winning their business.

Client: Any person employed by the institution or company that you either currently represent or have represented in the past.

Client Relationship Manager: A lawyer at your firm who has responsibility for managing the legal work and the day-to-day service relationships with a client. Most firms refer to these individuals as the "billing attorney" or "billing partner."

Contact Software: Computer software that allows you to store and retrieve vital information concerning clients and prospective clients.

Marketing: All of the activities that support your face-to-face business development efforts. Marketing activities create awareness of, and interest in, your services on the part of the client. Business development, through understanding the client's willingness to hire you, converts client interest to client action. (See Figure 2 on page 8.)

Needs: The acknowledged or unacknowledged legal, personal, or organizational desires or necessities of a client or prospect. Successful business development is premised on an understanding of these differing needs.

Needs Analysis: Undertaken in face-to-face discussions with the client and drawing on research, this is the process

Figure 2. Marketing and Business Development Flow Chart

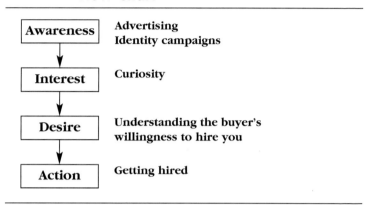

of determining the client's legal needs. In addition, other needs may emerge during your client needs analysis. These needs, of course, could be other than legal needs. They could also be needs related to how the law firm or you as an individual lawyer are servicing that client—that is, how you are managing the relationship. The effective and profitable management of these relationships will be critical to your long-term success.

Prospect: A potential new client whom you are not currently representing and whose organization or institution you do not represent.

Return on Investment (ROI): Your ROI is the profit you realize after subtracting your marketing and business development expenses from the revenue those expenditures generate. A positive ROI in marketing and business development should be a goal for every firm, yet the vast majority of lawyers and law firms fail to analyze their ROI. You may discover that your marketing and business development activities are unprofitable. Note that the ROI from marketing and business development to current clients versus seeking new clients is dramatically higher. Many consultants have calculated the economics to be ten times the cost and time to get the same amount of work from new clients versus expanding work from current clients.

Getting Started

"Never mistake motion for action."
—Ernest Hemingway

If, like many lawyers, you're tempted to rush headlong into business development by picking up the phone and making a lunch date with a prospect, my advice is simple: Don't. Sitting down with a prospect comes much later in the process—after you've thoroughly prepared in ways large and small that will dramatically increase your chances of success. Hastily seeking meetings with prospects and clients is, in Hemingway's words, to mistake motion for action.

Before you take to the field, you must know where you are, where you want to go, and what you need to get you there. As the following chapters in this guide explain, you must thoroughly assess the state of your firm's business, your resources, and the clients you wish to pursue within the context of your strategic objectives. You will need to put in place a business development framework, and, before anyone makes that first phone call, you must plan meticulously who your firm will approach and how. And before the first meeting, you must understand—and acquire—the business and interpersonal skills you will need to succeed. Through it all, remember: preparation is also an action. It begins with an attitude adjustment—displacing myths about business development with facts.

Myths Versus Facts: Reframing Business Development

From my work with lawyers all over the world, it's clear to me that many of them hold tightly to intensely negative beliefs about business development that reduce their effectiveness with clients or prospects. Many of these beliefs are simply mistaken, a combination of half-truths, myths, or professional lore that have no basis in fact. Under the spell of these myths, you are likely to dread encounters intended to win business and to evade, whenever possible, undertaking face-to-face meetings. Further, if you don't like to do business development, you are at the mercy of the buyer and your competition. Can you learn to like it? The answer is a resounding *yes*. Especially if you keep in mind this simple precept:

 How you think is everything. Reframe your beliefs about business development.

The discussion of myths and facts that follows is intended to help you do what cognitive psychologists call *reframing*. By substituting facts for myths, you can reframe business development more positively—and more accurately. Just as negative framing can be a self-fulfilling prophecy of failure, positive reframing can be a self-fulfilling prophecy of success.

Myth #1: Clients and prospective clients dislike business development and marketing.

Fact: Business development and marketing help clients and prospective clients understand how to establish and grow trusting, long-term relationships. Clients and prospective clients *want* to buy, but they emphatically do not want to feel that they have been sold. Most surveys of sophisticated clients reveal that the vast majority are interested in knowing more about you and your firm.

Myth #2: Business development and marketing are not part of the "true" practice of law.

Fact: Identifying and fulfilling clients' and prospective clients' legal needs are part of the process of helping people achieve their goals—to protect assets or to grow assets. Without business development and marketing, most lawyers would simply be "order takers," acquiring only the business that clients identified. You would also be doing clients a disservice by not helping them uncover other needs that they might not be fully aware of. Business development and marketing help identify additional opportunities for both the client and outside counsel.

Myth #3: Clients and prospective clients are seeking the smartest lawyer to do their work at the lowest price and I or my firm don't fit that profile.

Fact: Clients and prospective clients are, of course, seeking smart and cost-effective lawyers. However, they also want someone they trust, which may be the most important factor in their hiring decision. Bringing confidence, conviction, and passion about your clients and their organizations goes a long way toward overcoming their concerns about smarts and price.

Myth #4: It is the quality of the work product that determines the value of your services. Everything else is unimportant, comparatively speaking.

Fact: Clients presume that their current lawyers are at least as competent as their competition. Most clients and most lawyers cannot distinguish gradations of quality in work product from competing law firms. However, most people either know or can sense when they are not getting good service. Recent feedback from our clients during business development workshops indicates that their clients had the following concerns and expectations about outside counsel, in order of importance:

1. Commitment

2. Integrity

3. Competence

4. Fee issues

Proving commitment with new clients is always a challenge. Initially, by far the best way to prove that you will be committed to the client is through your references.

Myth #5: Rainmakers are born, not trained or created.

Fact: Business development skills are *learned* skills; they are not inborn. Daniel Goleman's work on "emotional intelligence" clearly indicates that the socialization skills acquired in early childhood create opportunities for individuals to become successful business developers and leaders. Conversely, can some people be viewed by their actions as client killers, death wish marketers, or droughtmakers? Sure. Nevertheless, even people who are viewed as client killers can learn business development skills and become, if not rainmakers, at least drizzlemakers. There is no reason that lawyers can't acquire business development skills if they are provided with such basic tools as a business development process and help with self-monitoring their conversations and body language in meetings with clients and prospective clients. You should consider attending a workshop on business development skills.

 People can be trained to be better at business development, marketing, building trust, and managing profitable client relationships.

Myth #6: Lawyers who need to do business development are probably not good lawyers, and that is why they do not have a solid, big "book of business."

Fact: The presumption that the most talented lawyers are busy and therefore do not have to do business development and marketing is simply not true. In fact, watching those talented lawyers make a point of doing business development even while busy brings to mind the words of President John F. Kennedy: "The time to repair the roof is when the sun is shining." We have also observed that the most talented legal minds also have a strong sense of how to interact with people and are always looking for new opportunities. Some of the best rainmakers we have ever seen compulsively seek new ways to help their clients and prospective clients. These individuals are passionate about their clients, their practice, and their firm.

 Passion is a great motivator and can play a significant role in helping you become proactive about your clients' needs.

Overcoming Negative Attitudes

In addition to the myths that abound about business development, other negative attitudes can also make seeking new business much more difficult than it has to be. Some of the most common of these attitudes, along with some suggestions for overcoming them, include:

"There is not enough time available to do the work AND get the work."

Suggestion: We as lawyers do what is urgent, not important. You may want to seek training on goal and time management. If your office looks like it has been hit by a paper blizzard with files and documents everywhere, then you are clearly a candidate for rearranging your priorities. If you want great work, you will have to find it. It will not fly through your window like a bluebird with a sack of gold attached to its leg.

"I don't like sales people; I don't like getting cold calls from brokers and financial planners, and I'm sure that my clients feel the same way about me."

Suggestion: How do you know how they feel about it? Have you ever discussed it with a client or prospect? Try asking them how they feel about lawyers who do business development really well—and what lawyers do in business development that puts them off. Many lawyers are professional, empathetic, good listeners and have great client care skills—some of the qualities that separate the winners from the others and that most clients greatly appreciate.

Successful business developers seek to understand the clients' needs before offering solutions. As Stephen R. Covey, the author of *The 7 Habits of Highly Effective People*, says, "Seek first to understand, then to be understood."

"I went to law school to avoid 'sales.' Some of my family members are in sales and they are too pushy and aggressive."

Suggestion: As a profession, we generally look down our noses at sales, business development, and marketing as being crass, boorish, unseemly, and unprofessional. Remember, however, that many clients have salespeople and marketers as part of their organizations and therefore recognize the necessity of business development. Further, they know that the best sales and marketing efforts deliver useful information that can be of great value to potential customers. In a larger sense, clients and prospects likely have to "sell" their ideas to their superiors, colleagues, suppliers, and investors. In fact, most of us are involved in selling in most aspects of our lives. Looking down on sales is therefore not only snobbish but also self-deluding. When you are in the field, however, it's helpful to distinguish between business development (offering clients a service because you know they need it)—versus sales (attempting to persuade clients to buy a service regardless of their needs).

"Our firm markets through numerous media and channels; I don't need to be involved."

Suggestion: Most lawyers and law firms spend far too much time and too many resources "broadcasting" solutions in hopes of finding a new client with the needs that correspond to the services the lawyer provides. They send out letters, client alerts via e-mail, newsletters, practice group descriptions, and firm brochures. They conduct new client seminars. They advertise. A friend of mine calls this the "smorgasbord approach." If you talk enough about what you do either face-to-face or using these other devices, perhaps clients or prospective clients can sift through the flack and find the silver bullet on their own. But don't bet on it.

"That's all well and good, but I have tried business development and marketing with poor results; it just doesn't work for me."

Suggestion: Read the remainder of this book, especially the chapters that provide a step-by-step guide to the business development process. Absorb the techniques you will learn there. Try them. You have nothing to lose but the false beliefs that hold you back.

The Right Behaviors and the Right Skills

Once you have reframed your approach and swept away negative attitudes, you will be far more receptive to making the effort to practice the behaviors and develop the skills that will enable you to excel at business development.

The right behaviors include

- thinking like a client;

- focusing on where you are likely to get business;

- acting energetically, remembering that, as the old adage suggests, "the early bird gets the worm"; and

■ developing empathy to understand and relate to the client's or prospective client's pressures, internal politics, budgetary constraints, management, and the risks they take in hiring you.

Above all, you will need to be persistent. Persistence is best defined as discipline. If the opportunity does not come immediately, don't give up. It may be "no" for now; however, through your persistence you can turn that "no" into a "yes" later.

The right skills include the ability to

■ establish face-to-face rapport in order to develop trust and long-term relationships;

■ write a concise, readable, and solutions-based proposal;

■ justify the cost of your services, providing the buyer with a business case for comparing cost and value received; and

■ negotiate in a manner that allows both parties to feel that they have benefited from the deal.

There's one final negative attitude that you should jettison immediately: "I don't have the aptitude to learn so many new things that lie so far outside of my specific legal skills." Nonsense. For more than thirty years, I've watched thousands of lawyers learn to practice these behaviors and develop these skills. So can you.

> **Rule:** Persistence can turn "no" today into a "yes" tomorrow. Never give up.

The Business Development Framework

"Luck is the residue of design."
—*Branch Rickey*

Business development entails two principal kinds of activities: 1) one-time activities to establish the overarching business development framework, and 2) recurring activities that constitute the ongoing business development process.

Taken together, the business development framework and the business development process constitute the business development *system*.

Before you embark on the business development process you must put the framework in place. A sound business development framework provides a strategic context in which individual development activities take place, assigns roles and responsibilities for business development, and establishes procedures for managing the process.

Start with Strategy

You can't effectively plan your pursuit of business with individual clients or prospects—that is, your tactics—unless you understand that pursuit in the context of the overall strategic objectives of the firm. A clearly articulated strategy can:

21

- appropriately and efficiently guide the work of the firm's lawyers and staff;

- efficiently allocate the use of scarce resources such as money, time, and skills; and

- send a clear message to the individuals who make hiring decisions so that they know exactly who you are and what you have to offer.

Unfortunately, strategy in many law firms has a troubled history that often takes one of two forms. The first is a tendency to over-analyze. Lawyers are by nature analytical and the endless possible strategic permutations of legal services, resources, industries, and geographies can lead to "analysis paralysis." The second is a tendency to formulate over-ambitious, inappropriate, or vague plans. Strategy can be heady stuff. It's exciting and often intellectually challenging to envision new markets, think of ways to rebrand in order to occupy a particular niche, or develop ambitious, if vague, visions such as "to be the law firm of choice in (fill in the blank)." In both cases, the result is the same: the strategy gathers dust on a shelf until it becomes clear that little has come of it; and then a new round of strategizing begins, often enabled by consultants who don't have to worry about implementation.

If the result of both these unfortunate tendencies is the same, the cure for both is also the same:

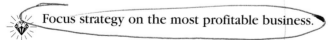

Focus strategy on the most profitable business.

In most law firms, 20 percent of the clients produce 80 percent of the revenue. Yet, typically they receive a minuscule portion of the firm's business development and marketing attention. Although increased competition, eroding client loyalty, "partnering," and a slew of other factors have caused some lawyers and law firms to re-evaluate key client retention efforts, most law firms do not focus most of their business development and marketing activities on client retention.

Willie Sutton, the infamous bank robber, may not be a proper role model, but he knew where the money was. Lawyers and law firms, on the other hand, seem compelled to focus their limited business development and marketing time and resources on where the money isn't—dispatching hit teams all over the place to give new business pitches to prospective clients, most of which will not pan out.

To be sure, natural attrition and other factors mandate that a firm keep looking for opportunities with new clients. But it's far more important to retain current clients. This is difficult for most firms to comprehend; that is, until a major client defects—or fades away. Then they realize not only how much of their revenue the client represented, but also the incredible amount of additional time and resources that must be devoted to getting back to where they were in revenues before the defection.

Given the realities of attrition and competition, the strategies of most firms will encompass some combination of retaining existing clients, expanding business with those clients, and finding new business. Further, firms will necessarily continue to position themselves—and sometimes reposition themselves—in the market for specific services or in specific industries. But no matter the specifics of each of those strategies, the underlying principle should be profitability. Do you want to concentrate your strategy on client retention? Then make sure they are *profitable* clients. Want to expand your business with them? Make sure it's *profitable* business. Do you want to capture new business in an industry you're not currently serving? Let profitability be your guide.

By providing a clear criterion of desirable business, a focus on profitability breaks through analysis paralysis and cuts through the fog of heady strategizing to create a clear bias for action. Moreover, it directs action toward what is, after all, the ultimate goal of any law firm: to make money.

Tightly Integrate Marketing and Business Development

Once you have a strategy in place focused on the most profitable business you should re-examine your marketing—all of the activities designed to create awareness of, and interest in, your services on the part of the client. Various surveys by consultants, the ABA, and state and local bar associations indicate that law firms typically pursue some or all of the following marketing activities:

■ bar activities;

■ public relations and community involvement;

■ speeches and published articles;

■ brochures and newsletters;

■ events marketing, such as prospective client seminars; and

■ entertainment.

However, we generally see law firms do these soft business development and marketing activities in an uncoordinated and unsystematic way. Often, individual lawyers in the firm are marketing themselves either as a boutique provider or as a low-cost service provider. It is far better to:

 Let strategy drive the allocation, design, and content of marketing efforts.

This means centralizing, or at least coordinating, all of your marketing efforts to win the most profitable business. Think of these activities as a portfolio of diversified investments from which you are trying to win the highest rate of overall return (defined as profitable business). Instead of taking a scattershot approach to the six activities listed above, for example, you can more precisely determine which activities to pursue, how to pursue them, and how to allocate your resources among them.

For example, bar association activities can raise your standing in the legal community, expand your credentials, and perhaps increase your visibility with clients and prospects. However, simply pursuing bar association activities for the sake of these general goals is less effective than making sure that those bar activities are directly relevant to your most profitable business. Further, the time and other resources you and your firm allocate to such activities must be pegged to the expected value they will have in the pursuit of profitable business.

The story is the same with each of the other typical marketing activities. Each has a general marketing purpose that should be sharply refined in light of your strategy. Speeches and published articles can demonstrate your thought leadership about a legal issue or your expertise in a specific legal service. However, you should choose your speaking venues and target publications in light of their relevance to your most profitable business. You may have a great deal of interesting things to say about torts, but if your most profitable business comes from routine business services rather than episodic litigation matters you are wasting your time and resources.

Brochures, newsletters, and other marketing collateral should be similarly targeted to your most profitable business. Too often, however, firms produce marketing material that is trying to be all things to all people, in the mistaken belief that you must be sure not to overlook any possible source of business. Again, it's worth remembering that 20 percent of your clients account for 80 percent of your business. You should target your marketing message and allocate your marketing communications budget accordingly.

Two typical marketing activities—events marketing and entertainment—merit special attention. Events marketing and entertainment are undertaken by lawyers and firms who understand that soft marketing activities such as bar visibility, public relations, and marketing communications are by themselves unlikely to consistently yield long-term profitable business. Such firms use events such as seminars for clients and prospects or entertainment to achieve the face-to-face contact that is essential for eventually winning or expanding business. Unfortunately, many of these active, visible firms nevertheless lack a systematic way to go about developing these relationships. As result, these elaborate and often costly efforts become little more than a series of dinners, lunches, outings, and other social events without any real focus on the client's needs. In other words, there is far too much selling taking place and far too little needs analysis— and selling is risky in a buyer's market.

More experienced law firms make a far more focused effort. They use face time and, in fact, many firms call it just that— "face time"—as a way of moving the relationships forward. They also use a great deal of teaming among the practice groups, geographic level or office focus, industry initiatives, and, of course, client-focused business development teams.

Many of these sophisticated firms, whether a one-lawyer firm or a 1,000-lawyer firm, also use client opinion surveys to determine performance of the overall firm in the eyes of the client. Such surveys not only help provide "quality control" and keep client satisfaction high, but also can be highly effective in securing face time to discuss issues uncovered in the surveys.

The way in which these sophisticated firms use these techniques points to a central tactical principle of all marketing activities:

 Design marketing activities to result in face-to-face business development opportunities.

All marketing efforts—from bar association activities to entertainment—should not only be managed with the strategic goal of winning the most profitable business but also with the tactical goal of converting these touch-points into highly productive meetings with clients and prospects.

Establish a Client Relationship Management Process

Leaving key client relationships unmanaged is likely to result in client defections, either partial or complete, especially if your competition is actively marketing to your key clients. Most well-established client relationships can sustain a litigation loss or a matter that exceeded the client's perception of cost. But they can rarely survive poor service in the form of missed client deadlines, phone calls not returned promptly, and other acts of neglect.

Often, the loss of a client is due not to a single catastrophic event but to a cumulative series of "little murders" committed by outside counsel. If clients do look for new outside counsel because of mismanaged relationships or neglect, then your survival demands a strong client relationship management process, with the immediate and long-term mission of client retention.

In addition, for both existing and prospective clients, a client relationship management (CRM) process can be used to track and share information from all client "touches," including

- mailings and other marketing efforts;

- encounters at speaking events, marketing events, and during the course of entertainment;

- phone calls;

- work performed and its outcomes;

- client survey results;

- business development meetings; and

- other contact.

This data, continually updated, provides a basis for planning and executing a sequence of carefully considered steps designed to win profitable business. For a one-lawyer firm this could simply mean maintaining a logbook of such data for clients and prospects and scheduling appropriate follow-up. For large firms, it could mean using CRM software with a central data repository for tracking client relationships and business wins and losses, and a system of prompts and other features to keep each relationship moving forward.

In multi-lawyer firms, the CRM system is likely to be administered by the firm's business management team, which is in the best position to coordinate the effort and assign roles and responsibilities in the business development process through which the firm will leverage the information in the system.

Reporting and Reviewing System

Finally, the business development framework should have a system for reporting on the business development efforts for each client and prospect and for periodically reviewing those efforts. The aim of this system is to establish accountability for business development. That accountability might take the form of an internal report either to you or to those partners responsible for the management of the firm's business. For example, in a firm using client development teams a periodic review or report on a specific client might contain the following kinds of information:

- the goals of the business development plan;

- updated goals;

- revenue for the team;

- projected current revenue rate;

- realization rates;

- practice group utilization;

- original practice group usage;

- current plans to expand to new practices;

- client's level of satisfaction with the firm;

- past, current, and continuous service improvement plan;

- what your competition is doing to take your work;

- resources needed in order to serve these clients effectively;

- how your team is getting along; and

- the next team meeting that would be required as a follow-up to the plan creation meeting.

Individual practitioners would of course simply omit the team-focused information.

Once the business development framework—including strategy, focused marketing, a client relationship management system, and a reviewing and reporting process—is in place, you can then turn to the business development process: the nuts and bolts of winning business from a specific client or prospect.

Rule: Strategy targets the most profitable business; marketing seeks to create face-to-face development opportunities for winning that business.

The Client Development and
Relationship Management Process—*Plan*

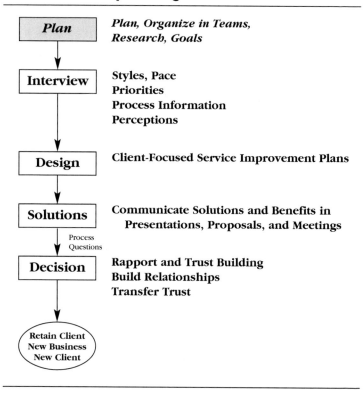

Plan — *Plan, Organize in Teams, Research, Goals*

Interview — Styles, Pace
Priorities
Process Information
Perceptions

Design — Client-Focused Service Improvement Plans

Solutions — Communicate Solutions and Benefits in
Presentations, Proposals, and Meetings

Process Questions

Decision — Rapport and Trust Building
Build Relationships
Transfer Trust

Retain Client
New Business
New Client

The Business Development Process: Plan

"Planning is bringing the future into the present so that you can do something about it now."
—*Alan Lakein*

Once the business development framework is in place you are ready to embark on the client development and relationship management process depicted in the accompanying chart. This chart, which you have seen before, represents the stages in client development and relationship management. As you move through this guide, you will find the stage under discussion shaded in on the chart and placed in the outside margin of each right-hand page. This will allow you to quickly thumb through this guide to review a specific stage in the process.

This repeatable, proven business development process provides a road map for client teams and individual lawyers pursuing business from existing clients or prospects. It can greatly help you manage your time, efforts, and resources. It also enables other members of your firm to understand where they are in the process, what steps remain, and what needs to be done in each stage.

With universal application for lawyers and firms of all types, this particular process has the added benefit of being useful in the following situations:

- finding, establishing, and maintaining relationships with new clients;

- deepening relationships with current clients for current needs as well as uncovering new opportunities in other areas;

- helping guide one-on-one relationships where the work might be of a personal legal nature, such as immigration, trusts and estates, white collar criminal law, and family matters; and

- helping multiple members of the firm develop multiple one-on-one relationships in a complex commercial, government, or institutional client or prospective client.

Know What You're Planning For

From a lawyer's point of view, many of the items in the list above are legal *services*. But from a client's point of view, they are legal *needs*, whether the client is aware of them or not. As Daniel H. Pink argues in *A Whole New Mind: Why Right-Brainers Will Rule the Future* (Penguin, 2005), the ability to understand the needs of others has become crucial for lawyers:

Much basic legal research can now be done by English-speaking lawyers in other parts of the world. Likewise, software and Web sites ... have eliminated the monopoly lawyers once had on certain specialized information. So which lawyers will remain? Those who can empathize with their clients and understand their true needs. Those who can sit in a negotiation and figure out the subtext of the discussion that's coursing beneath the explicit words. And those who can look at a jury, read their expressions, and instantly know whether they're making a persuasive case. These empathic abilities have always been important to lawyers—but now they've become the key point of differentiation in this and other professions.

As you go through the planning steps below, even though they involve inward-looking elements such as your firm's revenues and practice areas, keep uppermost in your mind that you're not simply trying to push a predetermined volume of services onto clients the way Detroit used to push cars into the marketplace. You're trying to fulfill the client's needs, whether those needs are unmet, unknown to the client, or are currently poorly served. Remember:

 The ultimate purpose of the planning process is to win a face-to-face meeting in which by having done your homework and listening carefully you can identify opportunities to meet the needs of existing clients and prospects.

Determining the needs of clients and prospects—needs analysis—is an ongoing activity throughout all stages of the business development process. In the Plan stage, you will initially put a stake in the ground about the client's needs based on your knowledge, research, and experience with the client and the client's or prospect's industry. In the Interview stage—perhaps the most crucial for needs analysis— you will explore client needs directly with the client. In the Design stage you will translate needs into how you plan to work together, especially with regard to service. Even in the Solutions phase, when you offer your proposed solution in the form of a presentation, you have an opportunity to learn more in the dialogue with the client about the presentation. In the Decision phase, you learn definitively what the client perceives as the company's needs and get valuable information about what those needs might—or might not—be in the future. At every stage of business development and throughout the duration of your relationship with a client, you should continually be refining the needs analysis.

Understand Market Trends

Planning begins with an understanding of market trends, a recurring part of planning because these trends can change and because your firm's relationship to those trends can change as your firm evolves. Understanding market trends can help you understand what kind of competition you face, where the greatest threats to your existing client relationships lie, and where the greatest opportunities exist for leveraging those trends with existing and prospective clients.

The chief competition and biggest threats to your business come from other law firms in your region, national firms, and foreign-based law firms in large U.S. cities. However, competition for large key clients may come from sources other than law firms. Contract lawyers hired as temporary in-house counsel may be, and frequently are, less expensive than outside law firms. Newly created research factories that turn out opinions on various legal issues may replace work traditionally done by your firm's associates. The client may also elect to keep more work in-house. Frequently, the client may create a new position—tax manager, in-house human resources manager, or environmental consultant—that reduces the outside law firm's opportunities.

The trend among many companies to consolidate their legal work with fewer outside law firms can also cost you business. This trend is reflected in the recent rash of requests for proposals (RFPs) and beauty contests where law firms new to a company as well as incumbent firms are being asked to go through a formal bidding process. These new "partnering" relationships are consistent with corporate America's trend toward downsizing and consolidating to fewer, more preferred suppliers.

Law firms will need hard facts about this trend, which are available from a number of sources. For example, a client may have already rationalized suppliers and vendors in other areas of their business, and the outside providers of legal services could be next in line for such pruning. Reports from consultants may also indicate that a company is likely to consolidate its legal services. Trends toward legal services consolidation in the client's industry may also be harbingers of things to come in the client's legal department. It's even possible that individual lawyers in your firm may be aware of coming consolidations, but the information hasn't been communicated throughout the firm. After all, most outside lawyers encounter more legal departments in a week than those legal departments encounter in a year. No one has a greater opportunity to pick up on these trends. Confronted with consolidation, law firms will have to be prepared to respond to potential client defections and competitive exposures.

On the other hand, the consolidation to fewer outside firms can also benefit you if you are one of the chosen few, because the client will have to rely on you and your colleagues to do the additional work that consolidation inevitably creates. You can seize this opportunity by creating a client-focused team that can handle the workload efficiently and create a strong bond with the client for the long term. You can even take the lead by suggesting consolidation to a client and seeking to manage it.

In any case, as you plan a business development effort, consciously review whatever trends currently dominate your market or are beginning to emerge. You will waste less time on fruitless efforts and will be armed with a superior tactical understanding as you undertake the next phase of planning—analyzing key client relationships.

Analyze Key Client Relationships

The best way to begin to analyze key client relationships is to create a computer spreadsheet of your top 150 clients. List the clients on one axis and the practice areas of the firm as the categories on the other. In each cell, show the revenue for clients by entering the fees collected yearly.

The spreadsheet example in Figure 3 shows a sample of a small firm that has taken its clients and organized revenue by client and practice area. This simple spreadsheet enables you to readily identify opportunities: you can quickly see which practice areas the client has been using, the overall fees collected annually, and practice areas not utilized at all. To further refine this spreadsheet, it may be

Figure 3. FLANNERY & FLANNERY, L.L.P.

Revenue
in $000

Client	Real Estate	Corp. Securities	Employ. Law	Environ-mental	Litigation	T&E Planning	Tax	TOTAL
Logic Solutions, Inc.	4	18	180		210		15	427
ABC Manufacturing	75	17	35	22	87		99	335
Strategic Systems	99	94			69		29	291
ZEO Computers	10	13	35	44		45	66	213
Lawn Games, Inc.					100			100
First United Bank			2					2
Total	188	142	252	66	466	45	209	1,368

necessary to include more detail. An analysis of the client's organization is helpful. For example, the client may have in-house lawyers assigned to product divisions or geographic locations. Each division or location may have broad-ranging legal needs. In such cases, the spreadsheet analysis should include both the overall company and each of its divisions. Also, practice areas of the firm may overlap. For example, a real estate transaction may also involve environmental issues, but you should be able to allocate revenues accordingly.

Start with a simple system and move to a more complex analysis later. By analyzing revenue or lack of revenue from various practice areas you may be able to pinpoint a potential client relationship problem or opportunity. Once this information has been collected and analyzed, it should form the basis for where, what, why, and how you will focus your business development efforts.

Segmenting the Market

Having analyzed your key client relationships, you are ready to segment all of your market. Most firms do not analyze the market for legal services based on buyer behavior and then segment the market accordingly. Instead, they write marketing plans based on what they want to sell, or they write individual, practice group, industry, or office marketing plans. However, market segmentation can be an invaluable tool for more efficiently allocating your marketing and business development efforts.

The chart in Figure 4 represents the market segmentation of a representative firm's book of business into three major areas: 1) key clients, 2) all other clients, and 3) prospective clients.

Figure 4. Market Segmentation of Sample Firm's Book of Business

Buyers	% of Firm's Revenue	Actions
Key Clients (Top 150)	80%–90%	Client-Focused Teams Client Team Leaders Technology Support ROI Analysis Client Opinion Surveys Business Development Training Client Service Improvement Plans Industry Knowledge Industry Conferences

Clients Other Than the Top 150
  Geographic Groups
  Practice Groups
  Individual Efforts
	5%–10%	Some of the Above, plus
		Association Memberships
		Speeches
		Articles
		Small Group Seminars
		Community Involvement

New Clients	??%	Referrals Cold Calls Advertising Identity Campaigns Industry Groups

This market segmentation chart identifies various types of buyers, the representative percentage of revenues associated with those buyers, and actions that would be "best practices" to achieve profitability.

The first segment encompasses key clients or those clients who represent 80% or more of your business. For many law firms, that would be somewhere around their top 100 to 200 clients.

The next category includes clients other than the top 150 or so. This segment can be further divided into those that fall into geographic clients (those located in places other than where your office is), practice groups, and your individual representation. Typically, this overall segment would represent about 5 to 10% of a law firm's clients.

The third group would consist of prospective clients to be secured through business development and marketing—the most difficult and time-consuming of all development efforts. The pursuit of new business also often involves ethical constraints, which may include strictures of the ABA and your state and local bar, all of which you should be aware of. If you're unsure about what is permissible, ask the appropriate bar for guidance.

To get the maximum return on investment (ROI) from each of these client segments you must tailor your actions to each, as depicted in the right-hand column. For example, business with key clients is best developed through client-focused teams and other high-involvement personal attention to this valuable segment. In the other than top-150 segment, you can develop business through more traditional marketing activities such as association memberships, speeches, articles, and community involvement. For the new client segment, you will rely on referrals, networking at business and industry conferences and events, cold calls, advertising, and a strong Internet presence.

Once you have completed the overall market segmentation analysis for your firm's book of business, you can then select the high-potential opportunities you want to pursue. For example, with regard to your top 150 clients you may consider a protect/retention strategy versus simply trying to expand your current business. If there is an opportunity to expand the business, the kinds of needs analysis that you do face-to-face with that client and through research will help you determine precisely where you might need to go over the next 12 to 24 months.

Having completed your key client analysis with respect to market share, you then want to look at all of your other existing clients and determine how much current market share you have with each. "Market share" in this case, as the Glossary notes, refers to the amount of business you get relative to the amount of money a client spends for legal fees with all other lawyers or law firms—a calculation also known as "share of wallet."

With the third category, prospective clients, you already know what share of wallet you have: none. Moreover, although the costs of acquiring new business vary as a function of how you go about it, the cost associated with acquiring new clients is substantially higher than getting business from current clients. In fact, cost analysis of new client acquisition may show that the cost of getting new clients is as much as ten times the cost to acquire the same business from loyal clients. Nevertheless, some lawyers make the fundamental mistake of pursuing new clients at the expense of neglecting their current loyal clients.

Despite these obstacles and pitfalls, however, experience has shown that new business development efforts can pay off. Further, you should think of your market segments in the way you think about a portfolio of investments in which you try to arrive at an optimal mix of long-term and short-term investments as well as investments with various levels of risk and return. Similarly, you should devote a certain percentage

of your development investments to new business in order
to keep the pipeline full for the long term and in the belief
that the payoff will one day be substantial.

Targeting and Prioritizing Clients and Prospects

Having analyzed your key clients and segmented the market,
you are ready to target individual clients and prospects for
your business development efforts. Targeting should proceed
according to the same strategic principle that drives your
overall marketing and development operation: finding and
keeping the most profitable business. For example, you may
want to target a key client most of whose business you already have in order to secure the remaining business so you
can lock down and protect for the long term what is already
a very profitable relationship. You should also target clients
for whom you already do substantial business and who represent a good upside opportunity for a substantial amount of
additional business. Target also the second-tier clients where
you have a small share of wallet but the potential to win a
substantially larger share.

To target prospective clients, you might identify those that
represent the most profitable business opportunity in your
geographic region, in your legal specialties, and in the industries in which you have expertise. You might also identify
targets in industries in which you have little presence but
which are likely to increasingly need your specialty. For
example, litigators might want to carefully consider the
pharmaceutical industry, which, for a variety of reasons, is
very likely to see more and more litigation in a number of
areas from product liability to intellectual property to com-
plicated contractual disputes.

In all likelihood, you will identify more targets than you have the resources or time to pursue simultaneously. Experience shows that the best way to prioritize the opportunities is according to the market segmentation: key clients first, second-tier clients next, and prospective clients last. Your first priority targets should be existing key clients for whom you believe you have an opportunity to expand the volume of the current services you provide or to provide a substantial volume of new services. Your second priority targets should be second-tier clients who, because of your expertise or looming changes in their industry or business, could be converted into key clients. Prospective clients remain the third priority, but should by no means be neglected.

By proceeding in that order you first hone your development skills with key clients, with whom you are far more familiar and with whom you are therefore likely to have more immediate success with the techniques described in this book. Those skills can then be systematically expanded to second-tier targets and, finally, prospective clients. Surprisingly, many lawyers and firms go about it backwards, first cutting their teeth on seeking new clients.

Once clients and prospects have been targeted, each will need an individual business development and marketing plan, including the needs and opportunities you have uncovered during the segmentation and targeting phases. Development for some clients and prospects can be handled by a single lawyer. Others may be so large that several hundred partners may need to take part in an effort to develop the client-specific plan; sometimes this may be accomplished through industry teams or geographic teams. In any case, the focus remains on the individual client and especially on the three crucial determinants of profitability:

1. the amount, measured in financial terms, of profitable work that comes or could come from these clients and prospects;

2. the number of areas of legal specialization you are providing and your ability to bring more of the firm's assets to assist with the client's needs; and

3. client loyalty and what drives it

Researching the Client or Prospect

Once you have targeted a client or prospect you should undertake research with one objective in mind:

 Find out as much as possible about the client contacts and the client's business.

Innumerable books, articles, seminars, and resources on the Internet offer guidance on conducting effective research to build a comprehensive knowledge base regarding clients and prospective clients before you visit them. Just a few of those resources include:

■ your law firm,

■ annual reports,

■ client publications,

■ industry conferences,

■ trade associations,

■ personal networks,

- consultants,

- other lawyers,

- SEC filings,

- business information services such as Hoover's and Dun & Bradstreet,

- the business press, and

- company Web sites.

Today, many of these sources of information are readily available on the Internet. For example, SEC filings through the EDGAR system can be found at http://www.sec.gov/edgar.shtml. (SEC filings can be particularly helpful because they require the company to explain the risks and liabilities in its business and any current litigation in which the company is involved.) In a matter of moments, a LexisNexis® search can turn up mountains of press coverage on a target client, often from local newspapers that in the old days of plodding through the *New York Times Index* or the *Reader's Guide to Periodical Literature* would certainly have been missed. And in the age of Google and other similar Internet search engines, you can often unearth useful personal information about your client contact simply by typing the contact's name enclosed in quotation marks in the Search field and hitting Enter.

- The purpose of this research is to understand in advance as much as you can about the person with whom you will be meeting and to be knowledgeable about the topics you will discuss—*not* what services you want to sell. By carefully researching the client in advance of a meeting, you will feel more confident, more comfortable, less reactive, and more focused on the client.

Most importantly, the research should be an ongoing needs analysis of the client or prospect, augmenting the list of needs you have developed during the targeting phase. Research should also give you some idea of the information you lack and should seek either through further research, expanding your contacts in the target company, or face-to-face interviews.

The next chapter will take up some of the essential needs analysis questions to ask in a client or prospect interview. Your research will not only help you frame these questions but also make you a much more acute listener when it comes to understanding the answers.

Thorough research of a client or prospect will also help you:

- understand how their business operates;

- make decisions regarding the client's financial position to determine whether legal services are in fact a return on their invested capital; and

- write concise, client-focused custom proposals and make concise, custom presentations about client needs.

With your business development plan in hand, including a preliminary needs analysis, and a meeting on your calendar with a client representative, you are now ready to encounter what many lawyers regard as the most daunting of all the steps in the business development process: the face-to-face interview.

Rule: Use research to help design client needs-analysis questions.

Success Story: A Client-Focused Team Wins Through Superior Planning

After losing a beauty contest for a significant piece of work, a large East Coast firm had just formed a fledgling client-focused team when it received an extremely comprehensive request for information (RFI) from the client's third party administrator (TPA) as part of a drive to control costs and reduce the number of outside law firms used. Millions of dollars worth of work were in play, and it was the client team's to win or lose.

Based on inside information gained through client "coaches" inside the organization, the team analyzed information garnered through the RFI process and began to plan for an impending request for proposal (RFP). Because of deep client knowledge acquired over the course of a long historical relationship with the client, coupled with the new team approach, the firm was one of 20 selected from a field of 120 to move to the RFP stage of the process.

The RFP arrived from the TPA. Faced with a daunting amount of information requested, the team allocated work and intelligence gathering among its members, each tasked to report back to the team with information. Because the client had prohibited discussing the RFP with client personnel, the law firm's client services staff gathered critical information by questioning the TPA. In just three weeks, the team, with the help of the client services staff, completed the 120-page RFP.

As a result of the proposal—straightforward, on point, and at full rates—the firm was one of eight selected for in-person interviews. With only a week to prepare, the team sprang into action: selecting representatives, reviewing the RFP, and rehearsing. Once again, client services staff was able to obtain important information from the TPA, even gaining the opportunity to observe the "lawyers only" interview. Each attorney was put on the "hot seat" during rehearsals and questioned by team members to refine responses based on anticipated interview questions. The group analyzed the viability of answers and reached consensus on important issues such as staffing and price. Of one mind, they became a real team.

Travel time was arranged to allow for an additional rehearsal at the client's location—an indicator of the firm's thoroughness that was not lost on the client. During the interview, conducted by three client representatives who were extremely familiar with the firm, the client mentioned the importance of the client-based team and omitted some questions because they said they already knew that the firm was well qualified. Following the interview, the client gave other firms the option to supplement their answers. However, client contacts told this firm not to change anything in its proposal. The result? The existing relationship with the client was expanded to adjoining states, with the potential work, billed at standard rates, likely to triple, while the relationship is stronger than ever.

The Client Development and
Relationship Management Process—*Interview*

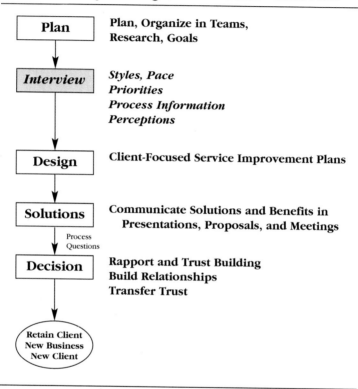

Plan	Plan, Organize in Teams, Research, Goals
Interview	*Styles, Pace* *Priorities* *Process Information* *Perceptions*
Design	Client-Focused Service Improvement Plans
Solutions	Communicate Solutions and Benefits in Presentations, Proposals, and Meetings
Process Questions	
Decision	Rapport and Trust Building Build Relationships Transfer Trust
Retain Client New Business New Client	

The Business Development Process: Interview

*"To listen closely and reply well is the highest perfection
we are able to attain in the art of conversation."*
—La Rochefoucauld

The objective of a needs interview with a client or prospect
is simple: to establish rapport, gain knowledge about the
client's business, and identify legal needs that your firm might
fill. Despite this apparent simplicity, many lawyers dread
these encounters and many others simply don't perform well
in them. In fact, lawyers' skill levels in interpersonal communications are possibly the lowest of all professionals we have
tested. Faced with those dual discouragements—dread and
poor skills—such lawyers could be forgiven if they adopted a
fatalistic attitude and simply accepted their limitations or left
the task to others in the firm. But, in fact, it's not necessary to
give up so easily. The skills required for successful needs interviewing can be learned. Even lawyers who are already
moderately adept at needs interviewing can markedly improve. To help you attain and sharpen those skills, this chapter will teach you how to:

- identify the different communication styles of different
  personality types,

- identify different styles of processing information,

- prepare a pre-interview plan,

- ask the 20 essential needs-analysis questions, and

- understand the real needs of clients and prospects.

It is well worth developing these skills because the face-to-face interview provides you with the means of getting to your ultimate goal of building and retaining profitable business. Well-conducted interviews enable you to:

- discover unrecognized client needs;

- establish rapport, build relationships, and earn trust;

- expand your contacts in the client or prospect organization;

- resolve the concerns or issues of existing clients;

- help clients achieve their goals;

- validate information about the client or prospect;

- gain a sense of their business;

- understand their hiring criteria; and

- learn about your competition.

Behind all of those benefits and the techniques for achieving them lies one overarching principle:

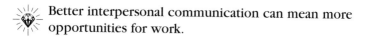 Better interpersonal communication can mean more opportunities for work.

Identifying Communication Styles/ Personality Types

INTERVIEW

In a seminal article entitled "The Power of Talk: Who Gets Heard and Why" (*Harvard Business Review,* September–October 1995), linguist Deborah Tannen observes:

> Communication isn't as simple as saying what you mean. How you say what you mean is crucial, and differs from one person to the next, because using language is learned social behavior. Although we might think that our ways of saying what we mean are natural, we can run into trouble if we interpret and evaluate others as if they necessarily felt the same way we'd feel if we spoke the way they did.

Different people communicate differently. They speak at different speeds, with different degrees of animation and different body language, from posture to eye contact to physical gestures. They process information differently, speak at different levels of abstraction and concreteness, use distinctive figures of speech or none at all, make imaginative leaps or stick closely to the empirical, and so on. In short, they *think* differently.

You are no exception. If self-knowledge is indeed the beginning of wisdom, your first order of business is to identify your own communication style. Understanding your style can then help you understand the style of clients and prospects and adjust your style accordingly. This is not a matter of attaining some chameleon-like ability to manipulate the client but a matter of communicating more effectively. There is no virtue in sticking rigidly to your communication style if you and the client or prospect are simply talking past each other. If little or nothing is communicated, it's a lose-lose: you miss the opportunity to understand the client's needs, and the client loses the opportunity to acquire what may be much-needed, valuable services.

But there's even more at stake than simply communicating effectively. By communicating in a style that takes into account the style of the client or prospect, you establish rapport and, eventually, trust—the essential ingredient of a long-term relationship. As Tannen says, "linguistic style is a set of culturally learned signals by which we not only communicate what we mean but also interpret others' meaning and evaluate one another as people." The basis for all successful business relationships is trust. Trust must be earned and earning trust with clients and prospective clients requires time, effort, focus, and empathy.

There are a number of tools that can help you identify your communication style, a number of which are listed in the bibliography. One of the most useful was first introduced to me more than 20 years ago by renowned presentations consultant/coach Barbara Miller of Barbara Miller Communications. Called "I-Speak Your Language," it is simple, quick, and accurate (available from DBM, Inc.). The tool asks you to select four different responses to a particular discussion you may be having with someone. These responses are observable behaviors and the self-scoring I-Speak questionnaire then helps you determine which of four distinctive personality types, each with a distinctive speaking style, you fall into:

- Intuitor,

- Thinker,

- Feeler, or

- Senser.

Each of these four communication styles/personality types, first identified by the psychologist Carl Jung, may be briefly described as follows:

Intuitors tend to be creative, innovative, big-picture types. They love new ideas; details bore them. They are often charming and friendly and tend to communicate openly, directly, and enthusiastically, jumping from one idea to the next. They are also often disorganized, impractical, and off-the-wall. According to Anne Field, about 13% of the population falls into this category ("Intuitor, Thinker, Feeler, Senser: Which One Are You Talking To?" *Harvard Management Communication Letter*, July 1, 2003).

Thinkers are rational to a fault. They are systematic, analytical, and demand empirical proof for anything under consideration. They are often perfectionists who are slow to come to a decision and who fear being wrong. They are introverted, highly cautious, skeptical, even suspicious. Their communication style is deliberative, indirect, and sometimes verbose. This group, Field says, makes up about 14% of the population.

Feelers are warm and friendly. They generally like other people and want to be liked in return. They focus on relationships and feel no urgency to reach a decision and can be patient, even passive. Their communication style is relaxed, indirect, and empathic—they are good listeners. This group accounts for about 30% of the population, says Field.

Sensers have a bias for action. Forceful, direct, and impatient, they want to get things done. They are practical, demanding, and decisive—and oriented to the bottom line. Their communication style is direct, blunt, domineering—they are extremely poor listeners. At some 44% of the population, they are, says Field, by far the largest of the four groups.

In addition to understanding your own communication style, you can also apply these categories to clients and prospects. Obviously, you can't administer the I-Speak exercise to them, but you can make an educated guess prior to the meeting based on your previous contacts with the person or by seeking information from colleagues or others who have had prior contact. And it is certainly possible, even during a first exposure to someone in an interview, to identify the person's communication style—and adjust your own accordingly to enhance communication.

How important is it to master this skill? Consider this: there is almost a one in two chance that you're going to be talking to a Senser—someone who doesn't listen well. There is a three in ten chance that you will be talking to a Feeler—someone whose feelings are easily hurt. For the unskilled, the chances are high that no communication or some damaging miscommunication will take place, leaving the client or prospect either uninterested or perhaps even alienated.

Identifying Styles of Processing Information

One of the most effective ways to understand which of the four communication styles you are faced with is to identify the way in which they process information. You can then not only adjust your communication style to establish rapport—friendly for Feelers, unemotional for Thinkers, and so on—but also to understand how best to present and exchange information.

This understanding of personal preferences in how to process information, says Dr. Paul Lisnek, an expert in the field of lawyer-client communications, provides the key to moving the lawyer-client encounter from rapport to trust (*Effective Client Communication: A Lawyer's Guide For Interviewing and Counseling*, West Publishing Company, www.PaulMLisnek.com). A model known as Neuro-linguistic Programming (NLP) provides a powerful framework for identifying those personal preferences. According to researchers on NLP, most people develop a preference for one of three dominant ways of processing information:

■ visual (sight, spatiality, mental images);

■ auditory (sound, speech, dialogue); or

■ kinesthetic (touch or feeling, body awareness, emotion).

Einstein, for example, first conceived his theory of relativity by trying to imagine what he would see if he were traveling at the speed of light, clearly a visual approach. Other people may "think out loud" in order to hear their ideas or they may engage in an inner dialogue—an auditory preference, even if it takes place silently in the mind. Still others may, for example, make decisions by way of "gut feel"—the kinesthetic. To understand the differences among these three preferences, think of the way you behave when presented with a new computer at work. Do you flip through the graphics in the quick-start instructions (visual), prefer to have your IT support person explain it to you (auditory), or do you boot up and dive in (kinesthetic)?

We all use all three of these systems from time to time and in varying mixes, depending on the circumstances. Nevertheless, in a meeting you can identify the client or prospect's dominant preference at the time through such cues as voice, gestures, word choices, and eye movements—and put them together with the four personality/communication styles—as follows:

Visual Information Processors

- **Voice:** They may talk quickly; the pitch of their voice varies from high to low and vice-versa. They paint pictures in their mind's eye first and then communicate those images rapidly.

- **Gestures:** They may gesture randomly, sometimes moving their hands as if they were drawing a picture. A business colleague of mine uses the back of the airplane seat ahead of him to draw imaginary flow charts to aid in communicating.

- **Word choice:** "Do you see what I'm saying?" You surely have experienced this very phrase in a telephone conversation with a visual processor. How could you "see" what they're saying over the phone? They are visual. They may use such visual metaphors as: "That's on my radar screen; let's focus on what is important; we see eye-to-eye on that issue." Visual processors may also start their sentences with the word "look."

- **Eye movement:** While speaking or listening, visual processors typically move their eyes up to the left or right, as if retrieving the visual image from their minds. It has been suggested by medical experts that this eye movement is driven by the visual cortex, which is in the rear portion of the brain, hence the eyes' need to seek the image by moving up. Some visual processors actually close their eyes while speaking or listening.

Visual processors tend to be Sensers, and their preference for the visual perhaps explains why they tend to be such poor listeners. Further, because visual images can often convey a great deal of information quickly, Sensers/Visual types are impatient with long explanations and lengthy reports. Flip charts, PowerPoint presentations, video, and similar techniques can be effective with these types—but only if the aids are truly visual. PowerPoint slides that are merely text/scripts, for example, are not genuinely visual and can be just as deadly in a conversation with these types as a long report.

Auditory Processors

- **Voice:** Auditory processors may sound like an FM radio announcer, speaking in a deep monotone with little inflection. They also tend to speak more deliberately and at a slower pace than visual processors.

- **Gestures:** Observing an auditory processor's gestures can sometimes give you the impression that they are playing an imaginary drum with their hands in front of themselves, rhythmically aligning words and gestures.

- **Word choice:** Auditory processors use auditory metaphors such as "I hear you; that's music to my ears; I'm tuning you out."They may start sentences by using the word "listen."

- **Eye movement:** Auditory types move their eyes from side to side on a flat plane.

Auditory processors may either be Thinkers, whose deliberate speaking style is connected to their reliance on evidence and analysis, or they may be Feelers, who rely on conversation to judge you. The difference can be significant, so it is important to use both frameworks—the personality types and the information processing styles—to identify which you are talking with.

Auditory/Thinker types are unmoved by visuals, which they often regard as unsubstantive. Staff lawyers often fall into this category—they want a full explanation of the options that are available in order to make the right decision. A general counsel however, who operates at the highest levels of the client organization and must understand many phases of the business, is likely to be a Senser/Visual type who wants to see the big picture.

Auditory/Feeler types prefer a dialogue in which they can hear your values, your sensitivity, and—in the context of buying legal services—some assurance that you will be a good fit with the client's culture. They will connect with Power-Point presentations but only if they are used as a means to dialogue, not merely as a script.

Kinesthetic Processors

- **Voice:** They tend to use the same FM radio voice as the auditory types.

- **Gestures:** They tend to have the same rhythmic patterns as auditory types; however, their hand movements are not outward but inward toward their body. They might typically look as if they were pulling you toward their chests or upper bodies.

- **Word choice:** "I feel your pain; that grates on me; my gut feel is; let's touch base" are some of the typical phrases they may use.

■ **Eye movement:** Kinesthetic processors look down when speaking or listening. Because they process information in a feeling-based mode, their eyes reflect the physical things they might be experiencing and hence look down at their bodies.

Kinesthetic processors tend to be either gruff Sensers who want to cut to the chase, or Intuitors who love big, innovative ideas. Again, by combining the two taxonomies here—communications style and processing style—you can identify which you are faced with. Entrepreneurial types, for example, tend to be Kinesthetic/Intuitors who are often so intoxicated with their own ideas that they're virtually blind to you and your ideas. If you're using visuals with them, put their logo on every page of your presentation (with their permission, of course), talk about your services only from their point of view, which is good advice when talking with any type of client, but absolutely critical with the Kinesthetic/Intuitor. Kinesthetic/Sensers are less self-intoxicated and are likely to be shrewdly sizing you up on the basis of gut feel. When talking with either type at the client site ask them how their company is organized and ask for a tour—there's nothing they like better than to be moving.

Some Notes of Caution

The cues on which the NLP framework relies apply to members of Western societies or other highly Westernized people. If you are interviewing a non-Westernized client or prospect—an increasingly likely prospect in the age of globalization—you should be extremely careful about using this taxonomy.

There is extensive research on NLP, and you will find in the bibliography additional resources for becoming more proficient in its application. For lawyers, the definitive text on client interviews, NLP, and the legal profession remains Dr. Lisnek's book. As you become proficient, remember:

 In adjusting your communication style, your goal is not mimicry, but to use learning methods and provide experiences that match people's preferences.

For example, with Visual/Sensers you don't need to parrot back metaphors like "let's look at the big picture," but in fact give that person something visual or something to visualize. Similarly, with Auditory/Feelers you don't have to begin every sentence with "listen," but rather make sure that you are genuinely engaging them in a dialogue, not subjecting them to a monologue.

Preparing the Pre-Interview Plan

Face-to-face meetings with clients for the purpose of arriving at a better understanding of their legal needs take two forms. The first is the full-blown, formal needs-analysis interview with an existing client or prospect, treated in detail in this chapter. The second, and often overlooked, form of face-to-face needs analysis should be taking place continually, interspersed throughout all of your encounters with existing clients. As you provide services to them—writing a contract, writing a brief, visiting a plant site—you should be constantly, discreetly asking them questions about their business, probing for unmet needs and opportunities.

 With existing clients, interviewing for needs should take place continually and concurrently with the delivery of services.

Before a full-blown needs-analysis interview, you should prepare a pre-interview plan. There is no virtue in "winging it."

And no matter your personality type or processing style, for this purpose you will need to adopt the analytical methods of the Thinker/Auditory type: in other words, write it down. Here is a basic pre-interview form that you can fill out well in advance of the client interview and review, if possible, right before you go into the meeting:

INTERVIEW

Pre-interview Form for [Client Name]

1. This interview was secured on the basis of:

    ❑ Existing relationship

    ❑ Referral

    ❑ RFP

    ❑ Seminar

    ❑ Marketing collateral

    ❑ Cold call

    ❑ Other

2. My objectives for this interview are:

3. My communication style is:

    ❑ Intuitor ❑ Thinker ❑ Feeler ❑ Senser

4. The communication style of the client or prospect most likely is:

    ❑ Intuitor ❑ Thinker ❑ Feeler ❑ Senser

5. The processing style of the client or prospect is mostly likely:

❑ Visual ❑ Auditory ❑ Kinesthetic

6. The pace of the meeting should be:

7. Supporting materials, if any, should include:

8. The priorities, goals, or concerns the client may have are:

9. Comments:

Item two—the objective of the meeting—is particularly important. Initial needs analysis meetings should be designed to gather information, share industry insights, and to secure subsequent meetings. To often, however, lawyers say "we have one shot with this client so we need to convey everything we can about the firm in this meeting." If you feel that you have only one shot, you probably haven't done your homework and will likely go into the meeting in "sales pitch" mode—and turn the client off. Take care to articulate your objective clearly and narrowly and to focus it on the client.

The form, if approached carefully and conscientiously, should help you to think carefully about what you will need to do to communicate effectively during the meeting.

Twenty Questions You Should Ask in the Interview

You've done your research about the client or prospect, thought about communication strategies, and completed

your pre-interview plan, but you may still be wondering:
What do I say? Where do I start? Here's where rainmaking
often turns into drought. Lawyers inexperienced in business
development often make the crucial mistake of assuming
that they're the ones who are supposed to do all the talking.
For lack of anything better to do, they start their sales pitch.
Or they try to convince clients or prospective clients that
the firm has a number of good lawyers who can help them.
Or more likely, they start with small talk as their way of trying to build rapport. For the first 45 minutes they focus on
sports, the weather, or subject matter that borders on the
trivial, and is, often, inappropriately personal.

But clients and prospective clients don't want a poorly
thought out sales pitch, and they don't need to be told about
your lawyering skills. They probably assume you're good at
what you do, or you wouldn't have gotten this far. And they
certainly don't want personal, small talk. They're as busy as
you are. What they want is to feel comfortable with you as a
professional and to see where you and your firm might fit in
with their business objectives. To make them comfortable,
you must get them to talk about themselves and their business objectives.

Your efforts should focus on listening to their responses.
The more they talk, the more you'll learn. And the more you
learn, the more natural the process becomes. In business development, information is always power—because it means
knowing what they need.

Knowing what to ask and how to ask is an art and a science.
The twenty essential questions proposed here are broad
enough to apply to most types of clients—both current and

prospective—yet specific enough to elicit the concrete information essential for effective business development. While many of these questions appear to target new clients, it is surprising how much lawyers don't know about the clients they've been serving for years. When those lawyers take the time to learn they often find that there is substantial business going elsewhere which, with a little effort, could be kept in the family.

First, here are a few basic rules:

- **Don't neglect the long-term perspective.** When they hear you asking about their plans three to five years hence, they begin to think of you as a 30-year ally.

- **Don't worry about asking new clients direct questions.** This is information they tell their brokers, their PR staffs, the stockholders, the press, and others in the business world. Further, they expect a high degree of confidentiality when talking to a lawyer, and they certainly want to talk candidly about their business because they want to trust their lawyers.

- **Ask current clients direct questions, too.** They will appreciate your interest and may even realize that such expert listening is the crux of delivering quality legal services.

- **You cannot and should not try to "sell" legal services to unwilling buyers.** Don't try to close the business at the first available lull in the conversation. Avoid the "sales pitch," as they may not be in the "catching" mode.

- **Never put them on the defensive.** Don't use the style of questioning you would use in a deposition or while cross-examining a hostile witness. The interview should be a win-win. The better they feel about talking now, the better they'll feel about hiring you later. Let them be the ones to bring up sensitive or painful matters.

- **Try to avoid the "why" questions.** Such questions are often received as judgmental, even when you intend no such thing. It's empathy and rapport that you're after.

- **Make all your questions as open ended as possible.** A "yes" or "no" answer will seldom do you any good. Phrase questions in such a way as to give them the opportunity to supply as much information as possible.

- **Don't feel you need to respond to everything they tell you.** Much of what they say should be filed away for future use at a more appropriate moment. Silence can help build informational savings accounts.

The needs-analysis process during an interview follows its own course and cannot be rigidly structured into a pre-determined sequence of the essential twenty questions or any other questions. In general, however, you may plan to start by asking general questions about their business: what products or services they offer and to whom. There's nothing they'd rather talk about. Then explore how they've structured their organizations. Finally, focus on their legal needs: how they've met those needs in the past and intend to do so in the future. In the course of that discussion, these are the twenty essential questions you will want answered:

1. What do you want your organization to look like in one year, two years, or five years?

This question is a good opener, because it allows buyers to begin talking about any aspect of their business they choose. But you also have your own tactical reason for asking it, which is to determine if they've formulated a strategic plan and, if so, what that plan involves.

Asking about strategic planning also tells you what kind of self-knowledge they have. Do they have a specific vision of what they want for themselves, or are they playing the field, reacting to events and market developments as they happen? Getting a feel for them in this way may tell you volumes about how they deal with every other aspect of their business, including hiring lawyers.

2. When and where do you plan to open new offices or plants?

This seemingly innocuous question is more than just a further refinement of the strategic planning issue. It will help you focus on a whole range of possible legal services, from real estate and lease negotiations to benefits planning for new staffs. In addition, it's information that will give you a real sense of just how aggressive and confident they are. It's one thing to talk about a strategic plan. It's another thing to state boldly, "We intend to open ten new branches in the next two years."

3. What new products, services, or major changes are you anticipating?

What if a retailer has decided that it wants to offer a discount brokerage service? You may have had no idea that the client or prospect intended to do this, and they may have had no idea that your firm has a securities practice. Here, the opportunity speaks for itself—thunderously.

4. What kind of research and development do you see as necessary for you to meet your strategic objectives?

Legal counsel is itself a form of R&D for clients, particularly where they will be breaking new ground. As they talk more about their plans—how much they plan to invest, and the kind of research they'll be doing—you may get a glimpse of your own future: the practice areas you'll need to develop to be at the cutting edge five or ten years down the road.

5. What is the profile of your typical customers and how do you market to them?

Getting a sense of who their customers are may help you determine how they themselves behave as customers. Are their buyers highly sophisticated and demanding, and to what extent? If so, they may want to see some evidence that you also treat your clients as peers.

Understanding how they market their products or services will naturally give you some clues as to how you should be approaching them. If they de-emphasize the direct pitch, maybe you should, too. But there's another reason to explore their marketing approach. How they structure their sales force, whether it's decentralized or pyramidal, and the quota pressures under which those salespeople operate, will give you crucial insights into their culture. What the company expects from its district managers it may also expect from you.

6. What are your employee relations concerns?

How they manage their sales force leads to a broader issue: how they manage their entire work force. This line of inquiry will strengthen your sense of their culture and its impact on their legal needs. Is it a paternalistic milieu or a demanding and confrontational one?

Querying their concerns here also will help accomplish two other basic objectives. First, it will indicate current or future labor/employee problems: collective bargaining, wrongful discharge, benefits planning, etc. Second, it will increase their comfort level with you. Whether they are a closely-held business or a Fortune 500 giant, there's nothing they fret about more—and nothing they'd rather talk over with a lawyer.

7. Who are your main competitors?

Here's another opportunity to get a sense of the business climate in which they are operating. Where there's an ongoing survival struggle with competitors, there are myriad legal issues, like commercial litigation, that the decision maker may not yet be pondering but ought to be. Conversely, less intense competitive environments may direct the client dialogue elsewhere.

8. What has the financial climate been like for your business?

Use care here. This is information you need to have, but the question must be presented in as non-threatening a way as possible. You don't want to put anyone on the defensive. And you certainly don't want them thinking you're worried about who's going to pay the bill. You're really trying to accomplish something very different. If they are in distress, they may want to think about spinning off a division, or even tapping your or your firm's bankruptcy expertise. Or perhaps you will eventually want to suggest custom-designed billing methods. You may even want to mention that you have helped other companies under the gun. Once you have a sense of where they are in the marketplace, shift the focus somewhat. Find out what makes them tick.

9. How are you organized, what does your organization chart look like, and who are the key executives?

You're really trying to gauge the organization's level of complexity. Is it a flat organization or hierarchical? Are there dozens of subsidiaries, or is it a one-cell organism? You don't necessarily need the whole organization chart, just enough information to know with whom you're dealing. You may uncover reporting relationships between their divisions or subsidiaries that you never suspected. The names of the key executives are also important at this juncture. You may never actually meet, say, the CFO, but you certainly don't want to sound ignorant later if that person's name comes up.

10. How are decisions made and who makes them?

Here, you're fleshing out the political underpinnings of the organizational setup. How bureaucratic is it? How autocratic? How many meetings will be needed before decisions, including retention decisions, are made? For lawyers in particular, it's vital to know who specifically makes the decisions. Is there a general counsel? If not, it may be advisable to minimize legal jargon in the face-to-face needs-analysis process.

11. What is the leadership style here?

This question will give them an opportunity to provide a wealth of insight into the personalities of the key players and give you a sense of those people before you meet them. You may learn that the leadership style emphasizes consensus-building. That's a cue to suggest setting up other meetings with as many of those important team players as possible. Even brief introductions are useful. The more decision makers you meet, the more opportunities open up.

12. Is there a legal department; how is it organized; what is its role?

Many sophisticated users of legal services have legal departments whose roles and officers vary widely. Obviously, you need to know, but be careful here. The general counsel may be out of the decision-making loop altogether. Let the client or prospect describe the role of their legal department and then you can draw your own conclusions. But ask to meet the members of the legal department in any event. There's no point in alienating your in-house counterparts.

13. What do you see outside counsel accomplishing for you or your organization?

Again, the question is broad enough so that the client supplies the essential information. Let them tell you what they want to buy, not just react to what you assume they need. They state their needs. You decide if you can fill them.

14. What recent uncertainties are affecting your business or what changes of any sort have particularly concerned you recently?

They have something on their minds; otherwise they wouldn't be talking to a lawyer. Some of them may want to jump right in and tell you about a serious problem that's been keeping them awake at night. Others will prefer to talk about bewildering regulatory, political, or market changes. But even generalities will highlight what they need from you today, as well as how you might be solving their other problems tomorrow and the day after tomorrow.

Depending on the answer, you may be on the verge of making an absolutely crucial determination: does this person want proactive counseling or crisis management? You're not going to use the same tone with a client who wants you to co-pilot long-range business strategy that you'd use for someone who needs you as a safety net. To know which tone will make them most comfortable, listen carefully to the tone they use with you.

15. What sort of legal services are you currently using, and do you expect any changes?

Perhaps they've been relying on outside counsel for, say, garden variety tax work or ERISA. If so, ask yourself why they're talking to you now. Maybe some new and critical situation is in the offing, and they feel the need to shop around. Or perhaps they're just dissatisfied with their current counsel and are looking to turn everything over to another firm.

This line of inquiry is also helpful because you'll be able to compare their current legal needs with the services they're now buying. Something may well be missing on the service end. With new or first-time buyers, there may be particularly glaring omissions. With long-term clients, watch for certain recurring patterns. Some of them may be turning to Firm X for, say, tax work, and to Firm Y for litigation. Do they even know that many firms offer the best of both? One-stop shopping is a powerful lure for most clients and prospective clients. Consolidating to fewer and fewer outside firms has been the most compelling "one-stop-shopping" trend in recent history.

For less sophisticated buyers, modify the questions. Ask them to imagine the best-case lawyer/client scenarios, as well as the worst.

16. What do you like about what other firms do, and what do you wish they would do differently?

Learn from your competitors' mistakes without attacking them directly. In fact, never make negative comments about your competitors. It reflects on the judgment of the buyer! Identify where competitors have fallen short in order to determine where you'll need to do better. It's helpful to find out who those other firms are, because they're likely to continue to compete with you for future work. The buyer may mention their names without your having to ask. This could turn out to be the most important question about your opportunity to replace the competition.

17. How much detail do you like to get from your lawyers?

Here is where you can get a real picture of their legal environment, and how much knowledge of the law they're bringing to the table. That knowledge will have a direct impact on your business development efforts. They may not be interested in hearing about all the details of your most recent case and aren't likely to appreciate your trying to dazzle them with displays of esoteric legalese.

By the same token, if they demand chapter and verse on every deal, they may well expect to be talking shop before they hire anyone. Incidentally, if they take pride in their legal knowledge, they probably have invested power in their general counsel, at least in determining which firms get what business.

18. How do you perceive our firm in particular?

You should be listening here to two things. First, what is it that has interested them enough to consider hiring you? Is it a particular practice area or your firm's overall reputation? Define that strength and, whatever it is, reinforce it in your discussions. But note also what even the most admiring clients fail to perceive about your firm. Remember, you're trying to build a long-term relationship. That means going beyond the one or two areas of expertise that they have seen fit to mention.

19. What criteria do you use in selecting lawyers? What makes a good lawyer?

A good lawyer may be variously defined as someone who wins cases, returns phone calls, respects in-house counsel, or keeps costs down. Sometimes they have no particular impression of you or your firm. They may just be spreading their nets, talking to as many lawyers as possible. So don't guess what they're looking for. Ask them.

20. How does your budgeting for legal services compare to what you spend on other resources?

Get a sense of the cost pressures beleaguering them. Sophisticated buyers aren't looking for bargain-basement rates, but they are attracted to lawyers who are sensitive to their need to stay within reasonable limits. Again, the main issue is their comfort level. They're going to want to know that you're someone they can deal with.

The last question you may want to ask is the one that will lead to a commitment. Building relationships is a process, and one in which clients and prospective clients themselves participate. So ask your client or prospective client for help in determining what the next step might be rather than begging for the business using antique "closing" techniques.

Understanding the Needs of Clients and Prospects

In addition to asking the right questions in the right way, you must be able to *hear* the answers—in all their manifold meanings. This requires active, empathic listening that picks up on the nuances of the conversation—the implicit as well as the explicit content. Ostensibly, you are listening in order to discover the client's legal needs, but such needs are inextricably bound up with other acknowledged or unacknowledged personal or organizational desires or necessities. Successful business development is premised on an understanding of these differing needs and the ability to discern them in client conversations. Those needs include:

- **Active Needs:** These are the client's legal needs that you and your competitors may currently be servicing.

Typically, these are matters that the client has hired outside counsel to address and they usually involve a pre-existing condition. Often, the client already has a price in mind when hiring. The client also usually has a buying process in place such as a short list, or a formal request for proposal (RFP) process, or competitive presentations from firms being considered. This recurring and possibly routine work can vary from the highly complex to commodity legal matters.

These kinds of needs are often made explicit at the outset. A franchiser, for example, may simply say, "We're about to move aggressively into your geographic area and we need an experienced, reasonably-priced firm to handle all of our real estate closings there."

- **Visionary Needs:** These are legal needs that the outside counsel is not aware of and which have not yet emerged as active needs. Confidential and client-driven, visionary needs might take the form of a refinancing, a bankruptcy, or an initial public offering (IPO). The client's buying criteria are usually well-developed in advance of hiring outside counsel to address these needs.

These needs may be stated more or less explicitly by a long-time client. Prospects, however, may be reluctant to reveal these needs quite so explicitly on first meeting and may be quite circumspect, especially where the information is highly sensitive from an investment point of view. The prospect may simply ask you to talk generally about your firm's experience with large organizational and financial issues, or they may be interested in your work with specific clients along those lines without telling you exactly why they're asking.

- **Latent Needs:** These are legal needs that clients or prospects do not realize they have, yet you, as outside counsel, clearly recognize. Typically, if you discover these needs in a face-to-face meeting, the client will be less price-sensitive to them than to active or visionary needs and may hire you at the time these latent needs become apparent.

- **Ego Needs:** These are clients' personal or psychological needs, such as the need to feel that they have been listened to. Buying your legal services is something that they may enjoy and understanding their ego needs facilitates the growth of the relationship. Behind what they explicitly say, you may detect them saying, in effect, "I need to feel important," or "I need to be consulted about major decisions."

- **Organization or Company Added-Value Needs:** These are needs that you go the extra mile to meet even though the actions that you take to identify and fulfill them are not billable. Examples of such actions include helping them find people, money, customers, suppliers, deals, referrals, and the like.

- **Job Needs:** Clients or prospects may need to look good to their immediate superiors. These needs, if they are met or exceeded, may result in a promotion, a bonus, or some other recognition for the client. From the client's point of view, these may be the most important needs of all. In effect, they are saying, "Make me look good" or "Your legal work, done well, will get me a larger annual raise."

- **Implied Needs:** These are needs that lie behind another need. You must uncover them in your discussions with clients. For example, a client asks you for a discount off your standard rates. Does the client need to achieve lower costs, or is there something else going on? Through further conversation, you may discover that the real need is not economic but the client's need to show her superiors that she was able to win a concession from you regarding fees. Or suppose a client asks you if you have an office in Austin, Texas. Rather than trying to sell some solution against an unknown need in Austin, you should find out exactly what their needs in Austin are. The appropriate response would be, "No, we do not have an office in Austin, Texas; however, what are your needs there?"

As I have noted, these differing needs can be combined in ways that require a sophisticated weighing of motives, business conditions, and legal considerations. A new CEO contemplating such a visionary need as a major restructuring may be as driven by an ego need to take a bold stroke as by business necessity. An active need for routine legal services may also be driven by the decision maker's job need to hold the line on costs.

Through solid research, careful preparation, acute interpersonal skills, and active listening, you have by this point developed a sense of the organization's operating environment, the personalities, and their decision-making styles. Any number of things might happen next. You may meet with other key executives. Ideally, you will soon be asked to prepare and present a formal presentation, written, verbal, or both—the next steps in the business development process.

Rule: When interviewing, listen and don't pitch.

Success Story: Winning Trust Through the Initial Interview

A partner in a medium-sized Midwest law firm received a call from the CEO of a NYSE company headquartered in the area who was looking for a new firm to serve as outside general counsel. The CEO asked if he could interview the partner. The partner, who had recently completed training with the author of this Field Guide, quickly responded that, in her experience, a brief meeting with the CEO and possibly other senior managers to get an understanding of the company's needs and goals would be a productive next step. The CEO agreed to spend an hour with the partner "just talking" about the company, its strategy, and legal needs in order to allow the partner to prepare a presentation and team that could best address those legal needs.

Instead of talking for only an hour, the CEO and the company's other executives at the meeting enthusiastically talked about their business for two hours. Armed with detailed information about the specific legal needs of the company gathered at the meeting, the partner assembled a team with the skills and personalities that best fit the needs and the management style of the company. Most importantly, the partner was able to learn the motivation—a broken relationship with existing counsel—for the CEO's seeking a new relationship and to understand that his most important goal was to find counsel that he felt could be a trusted partner in achieving the company's aggressive strategic plan.

A week later, the partner and her team gave a formal presentation to the CEO and CFO of the company. All of the lawyers had been briefed on the partner's previous conversation with the CEO and were sensitized to his priorities. Two days after the presentation, despite competing with several higher profile firms, the partner received a call that the firm had been selected. In communicating the decision, the CEO made a point of saying how impressed he was that the firm was the only one that took the time to find out what the company was looking for and specifically addressed their needs instead of trying to sell the firm.

INTERVIEW

The Client Development and
Relationship Management Process—*Design*

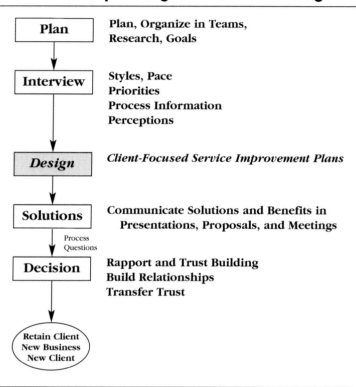

Plan → Plan, Organize in Teams, Research, Goals

Interview → Styles, Pace
Priorities
Process Information
Perceptions

Design → *Client-Focused Service Improvement Plans*

Solutions → Communicate Solutions and Benefits in Presentations, Proposals, and Meetings

Process Questions

Decision → Rapport and Trust Building
Build Relationships
Transfer Trust

Retain Client
New Business
New Client

82

The Business Development Process: Design

"He profits most who serves best."
—*Arthur Sheldon*

As a result of your client-needs interviewing, you should be ready to design a legal services improvement plan that is tailored specifically for the client. Outside counsel typically receive written materials from in-house counsel called "Guidelines for Outside Counsel." However, developing a service plan is different from simply responding to these guidelines. You should take a far more proactive approach and design a service plan that exceeds the expectations of the client and offers ways to serve that the client had not considered. *The result:* a service plan that sets you apart from the competition.

To help you achieve this critical goal, this chapter encompasses:

■ the essential elements of a service plan;

■ differentiating on the basis of service;

■ making service visible, tangible, measurable; and

■ examples of extraordinary services.

The objective is to learn how to design these plans specifically and then to understand how to use extraordinary service as a competitive strategy.

Throughout this stage of the process, you should stay sharply focused on the specific client. A very large financial institution, for example, would have different needs with regard to service than a small rural bank. One sure way to lose focus is to jump ahead to the presentation step in the process:

 Do not confuse designing the service plan with crafting the client presentation.

Far too many people conflate the two steps. They develop the plan entirely in PowerPoint, put a title slide on it, introduce it with the firm's boilerplate, weave in some running agenda slides, append a "Questions" slide and—voilà—they've killed two birds with one stone. In fact, you're likely to miss *both* birds and end up designing an inadequate plan and creating a slapdash presentation. At this stage, you should stay focused on the substance of the plan, not on how you will present it.

The Essential Elements of a Service Plan

During the needs interview you've explored the business environment and legal needs of the client or prospect. They may have told you explicitly what those needs are, and through your careful questioning and acute listening you may have deduced additional needs—implied, visionary, organizational, or others. Moreover, you should have learned what they liked and didn't like about what other providers of legal services delivered and what those providers should have done differently. From all of that information, you should be able to construct a highly client-specific service plan that will really drive the working relationship for both parties.

As the familiar Rotarian motto at the head of this chapter suggests, the watchword for this stage of the business development process is *service*. That doesn't mean you should simply make general affirmations to the client such as "We will provide excellent service at all times." First, it requires that you understand and keep firmly in mind some fundamental differences:

 Distinguish between legal services, value-added services, and service quality.

Legal services are the specific legal tasks you are proposing to deliver—from writing contracts to handling litigation to performing legal due diligence on mergers and acquisitions to providing general legal advice. Value-added services may include helping the client find people who can help them, helping the client to find sources of financing, connecting clients with customers or suppliers, bringing them business opportunities, referrals, and the like. Service quality covers not only the quality of your legal services and your willingness to add value at no extra cost, but the efficiency, responsiveness, and trustworthiness with which you conduct every aspect of the client relationship. So when you're promising to provide "excellent service" ask yourself whether you mean that the quality of the legal work will be excellent (legal services), or that you will go the extra mile (value-added services), or that you will take care of the client's needs efficiently, promptly, and effectively (service quality).

Second, once you have those distinctions clearly in mind, you can then consciously integrate them into a carefully thought out plan that will set you apart from the competition. Based on the needs analysis and any input from the client about his or her expectations, the plan should include these essential elements:

- specific legal services to be provided;

- services that add value to the client organization or the client's personal agenda;

- plans for maintaining high-quality service delivery;

- demonstrated improvement over the past in any or all elements of service;

- unique client focus throughout;

- implementation plans, including specific action steps, dates, and responsibilities; and

- a written service plan, as opposed to an oral proposal, to be presented to the client.

The plan, especially all of the service initiatives, should be created by a client-focused team drawn from throughout the parts of the firm that are relevant to the client and the firm's overall service execution. The client-team approach ensures that you will be able to deliver what you promise and deliver it in an extraordinary way. And it heads off the possibility of other members of the firm unintentionally acting at cross-purposes with the best interests of the client or the firm's relationship with that client.

Differentiating on the Basis of Service

In a typical competitive business development scenario, the prospect or client presumes that you are capable of doing the work; otherwise, the prospect would not be talking with you or the existing client would not have hired you. Where there is no measurable difference in the work product quality between competing firms then the quality of client service becomes the differentiator.

DESIGN

How important is the quality of service? Research shows that lawyers lose clients as a result of poor legal results and costs only about 10 percent of the time. Overwhelmingly, surveys of clients suggest that quality of service plays a far bigger role in the hiring and retention of outside counsel. Clients have typically ranked commitment and integrity as their number one and number two expectations of outside counsel, while competence ranked third and fee issues ranked only fourth. Commitment and integrity, of course, are intimately bound up with the quality of service, while competence, legal services, and fees—last among client concerns—have little to do with quality of service.

More negatively, some recent surveys of clients indicate that the vast majority, as much as 70 percent, are dissatisfied or uncomfortable with some aspect of outside counsel's service delivery. This dissatisfaction may result from such simple sources as the failure of outside counsel to return phone calls, forward documents on time, or be adequately prepared for meetings.

Most studies also indicate that understanding the client's business holds the key to providing extraordinary service. Your careful planning, research, and needs interviewing should have provided you with the requisite understanding. However, you have to translate that understanding into value-added services and service quality as well as legal services. A thorough understanding of the client's business should suggest particular value-added services, such as recommending candidates for a key executive post, or helping them select consultants to address a specific business issue. In addition, an understanding of the client's business and organizational structure can help shape the quality of your service delivery, such as providing periodic reports to key decision makers or timing legal consulting to coincide with milestone events in the client's industry or business.

Making Service Visible, Tangible, and Measurable

Once you have formulated your service initiatives, settled on demonstrated improvements over the client's past experience, and established timelines, roles, and responsibilities, you should make the detailed service plan visible, tangible, and measurable to the client.

Visibility is a matter of putting the plan in writing, where appropriate, in order to provide it to the client. Surprisingly, many firms fail to provide such detailed, client-focused service plans, relying instead on oral proposals, rudimentary retainer contracts, or presentations. In addition, the plan should include a projection of costs—not simply a statement of hourly rates.

Tangibility is the determination to use the written service plan as a living document with the client. Make it clear in the plan itself that the plan will be communicated constantly in meetings and periodically revisited in order to maintain client focus and provide a framework for continually refining the relationship.

Measurability provides the client with the concrete means for tracking your performance, providing feedback, and ensuring accountability. For example, the listing of the specific roles and responsibilities of members of your firm provides the client with the ability to track individual accountability as well as the performance of the firm overall. The plan itself can be used as the basis for periodic reviews of your performance and easily converted into a report card for that purpose. The measure phase of the plan can also include the use of such tools as the Quality Grid (see Figure 5).

By ranking the quality of the firm's work product on one 0 to 10 axis of the Quality Grid and firm-wide service quality

Figure 5. The Quality Grid for the Entire Firm

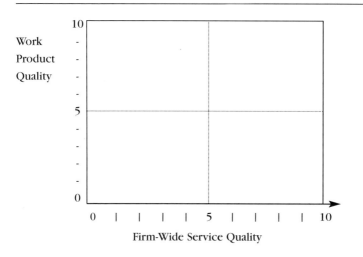

Work
Product
Quality

Firm-Wide Service Quality

on the other 0 to 10 axis you can arrive at the quality level for the *entire firm*. But before using this tool with a client, the firm should first do an internal assessment, if possible, with lawyers throughout the firm participating anonymously. If the exercise turns up wide variation within the firm with regard to performance, it can be a signal of vulnerabilities in your client relationships. (We have found that most firms rate their work product between 6 and a 9.5 and their service between 5 and 9.) Later, when you ask clients to rank you on the Quality Grid, you can compare their assessments with your internal assessment and, if you're not in the upper right-hand quadrant in the client's eyes, you can find out what you need to do to get there.

You might also undertake periodic client satisfaction surveys and other feedback exercises. (See *Appendix B:"Opinion Surveys Can Help Firms Keep Clients Happy."*) Once these measurement mechanisms are in place, they can provide you with an early warning system about potential trouble in the client relationship and about opportunities for additional work.

By making your service plan visible, tangible, and measurable you signal both your confidence in your firm's ability to deliver and your willingness to be held accountable at all times—traits that the client is likely to find highly attractive. According to studies that we have seen over the years, the team leader or billing lawyer typically makes a promise to the client to provide high-quality work product and service. Typically these promises have been oral. By making them visible, tangible, and measurable, you can ensure that the internal law firm team that touches the client— even if that team consists of only one lawyer and a paralegal or secretary—understands completely what has been promised.

Examples of Extraordinary Service

To achieve extraordinary service you can start by beginning every new relationship with a strategic assessment of the client's needs. Let them know that you would like to spend a half-day at their site to really understand their business and their business goals. This will help your ability to develop an even more focused client service plan and it will let them know that you take serving *them* specifically with the utmost seriousness. Also make it clear that you are not charging for this service—your learning curve costs should be built into the relationship.

Now that you understand the client's business, think carefully about opportunities you have to go the extra mile—and describe them explicitly in the written service plan. For example, you may want to make it clear that you intend to keep the client informed about the status of legal matters through periodic written reports, quarterly presentations, project management software, and regular e-mails. You may also state your intention to provide continuing legal education, in-house seminars, periodic executive briefings on key subjects, newsletters, and client alerts conducted by partners who go to the client's location and update them as to what changes in the law might affect their business.

You can also use budgeting tools and spreadsheets to help them forecast the costs they might incur. Such financial tools are especially valuable in estimating the cost of litigation. Consider also offering to tie their information and technology systems, such as e-mail, documents, document transfers, electronic billing, and research databases together with yours so that they can communicate easily and efficiently. You might even create an extranet between you and the client for managing complex litigation, mass torts, or all of

the client's business with the firm. You can also use your resources and your staff to help clients become more effective
and efficient, including training their people on doing more
work on their own. Although you may lose some billable
hours, you are likely to more than make them up through
the other work that a solid, long-term client relationship
brings as a result of such services.

You can also provide some of the additional value-added activities previously discussed that do not normally fall under
the classic definition of practicing law. Bring more resources
to the table, such as consultants or lawyers that could assist
the client in their business efforts. You might identify for
them customers or additional suppliers. You might help
them find money if they are looking for funding. You might
even have your marketing and business development people
assist them with their marketing and business development
mission. Take your business development and marketing
people on early visits to the client to demonstrate your commitment to perform to the best of your ability as a firm.

Through the explicit promise of these value-added services
and high-quality execution in your service plan you dramatically differentiate your firm. Let the client know that your
client team will meet periodically to discuss the client's business but not charge for the time. One of the things clients
ask for most is value for the dollar, which these services certainly provide. But in order to communicate that value, you
must master the skills required for the next step in the business development process: presenting your solution to the
client or prospect.

Rule: Make the invisible—service—visible, tangible, and
measurable.

Success Story: Designing Specific Service Initiatives Tailored to the Client's Aspirations

A top ten international law firm reached out to partner with a European energy client that was transitioning from a regulated business structure to a deregulated world market environment. The law firm assembled a world-wide client services team built around the client's future business model. The client was then invited to participate in a joint planning session to help design a client service improvement plan aligned around the energy company's strategic goals.

This collaborative design approach enabled the client and the law firm to integrate their people, processes, and technology into a dynamic service team that was able to respond more rapidly to the client's needs and to the threat of competition and to introduce innovative legal solutions more quickly. With the seamless, global support of a legal partner who knew where the client's business was going, the energy company successfully transitioned to an unregulated business model. And the law firm won the business and the loyalty of a long-term, major client.

DESIGN

The Client Development and
Relationship Management Process—*Solutions*

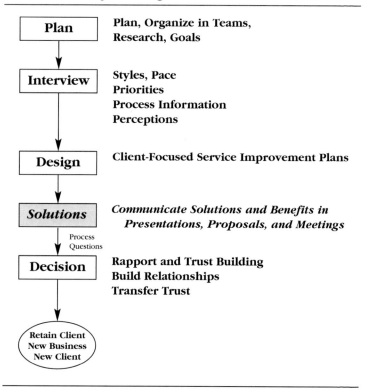

Plan	Plan, Organize in Teams, Research, Goals
Interview	Styles, Pace Priorities Process Information Perceptions
Design	Client-Focused Service Improvement Plans
Solutions	*Communicate Solutions and Benefits in Presentations, Proposals, and Meetings*
Process Questions	
Decision	Rapport and Trust Building Build Relationships Transfer Trust
Retain Client New Business New Client	

94

The Business Development Process: Solutions

"We are generally the better persuaded by the reasons we discover ourselves than by those given to us by others."
—*Blaise Pascal*

The presentation is the culmination of all of your efforts—your careful planning, needs analysis, and solution design—and largely the determinant of whether you win the business. Like all of those earlier stages, the Solutions stage requires careful planning as well as execution. There is no all-purpose template for such presentations, only general guidelines and the lessons of experience; and there is no one-size-fits-all style of delivery, only a range of possibilities geared to the specific needs and learning style of the client or prospect.

Most importantly, this stage is not synonymous with the presentation document. Rather, the Solutions stage is a process that includes pre-presentation work, delivery of the presentation, and post-presentation work. To help you through that process, this chapter covers:

- planning the presentation,

- a checklist of essential elements of the presentation,

- weighting the elements,

- adapting the presentation to the client's learning style,

- delivering the presentation, and

- following up on the presentation.

Planning the Presentation

Planning the presentation begins with an understanding of
the context in which you are seeking the business. There are
several potential scenarios here:

1. The client is currently going through consolidation of
   the number of outside firms and has decided to put
   your name into the pool that will bid for the work.

2. You have conducted client needs-assessment interviews and found opportunities for additional business
   in your practice area.

3. You have found additional opportunities in practice
   areas other than your own.

4. You have received a request from a potentially new
   client to compete for work.

Each of these scenarios requires a carefully tailored response.
For example, if the client is consolidating the number of outside firms, you should be acutely aware of the competitive nature of the exercise as you craft your presentation and be
sure to differentiate your firm through service and the quality
of the existing relationship, not just cost. If the goal is to expand business in your practice area, the focus should fall on
client needs—whether implied, visionary, organizational, or
others—and the business value to the client of having those

needs met. If the goal is to expand business in practice areas other than your own, your presentation will to some degree resemble the type of presentation you might give to a prospect—especially if the client decision makers differ from those you have dealt with in your own practice area. Finally, a presentation to an entirely new prospect will tend to be more comprehensive than other presentations in every respect—about your firm, the client's needs, and your differentiators.

Regardless of which scenario you find yourself in, the key to success at this stage of pre-presentation planning lies in a simple, but powerful, principle:

 Involve the client or prospect as a coach on how you should present your solutions.

For example, you might find an individual within the client or prospect organization who agrees to be your coach and will help you craft the presentation so that the message is precisely relevant to the listeners. Short of finding an outright champion, you can ask a series of questions prior to giving your presentation or sending your proposal that will get the client or prospect directly involved in the planning. Not only will their involvement help ensure that your presentation truly addresses their needs and in the way that they prefer, but also—as the quotation above from Pascal suggests—it will give them some stake in the contents that can lead to their ultimately receiving your ideas as if they were their own.

Some key substantive and procedural questions include:

■ How might we best address these challenges and concerns that we've been discussing or that you have asked us to present?

- What additional information might you need before we present?

- How should we submit the written proposal?

- Would you like to review our presentation or proposal before we present it?

- Are other firms presenting and, if so, how many?

- What are the other firms doing?

- Will we be the first, middle, or last to present?

- Who will attend from your group?

- How will the decision be made?

- Will the decision be made immediately, and if not, how long will it be until the decision is made?

- If we are successful or unsuccessful, how appropriate would it be for your people to debrief us as to how the decision was made?

In addition, you should also ask the relevant questions about *how* to present:

- How are important ideas and solutions presented in your organization?

- How do your executives present to each other?

- How long do we have to present?

- What will be the format for this presentation or proposal?

- What will the meeting room look like, and may we look at it?

A Checklist of Essential Elements

Before you begin weaving together all of the various strands of the presentation, you should be aware of the essential elements that you must include:

❑ a theme or overarching message;

❑ an overview of the client's needs;

❑ a client-specific service improvement plan for meeting those needs;

❑ a benefits discussion that differentiates your firm on the basis of legal services, value-added services, and quality of service;

❑ implementation plan—schedule, calendar, or charts showing dates and tasks;

❑ previous successes and references that closely match their needs and your proposed solutions;

❑ fees and cost ranges (not just hourly rates);

❑ administrivia—office location, etc.;

❑ names, telephone numbers, and biographies of the proposed service team; and

SOLUTIONS

❑ summary, recommendation, and a discussion of next steps.

Depending on the client and the context, the order and the inclusion of these elements may vary, as will your use of agenda slides and other structuring devices, but in no case should you omit the benefits case, differentiators, and an understanding of the next steps.

Weighting the Elements

The weight you give to each of the essential elements in your presentation will also vary according to where you stand with the client or prospect. There are three distinct stages in competing for work:

1. competency level;

2. comparative performance; and

3. differentiation.

In stage 1, the buyer looks for the technical capabilities of the lawyer and the reputation of the firm. If the client or prospect believes that you have the requisite competencies and holds your firm in high regard, then you should give more weight in your presentation to the level of *comparative performance*. Emphasize your credentials in the industry and in matters that are similar to the needs of the client and present your track record compared to that of other firms. If you have met the criteria for superior comparative performance, then emphasize your *differentiation* on the basis of value-added services and quality of service.

Differentiation would include a mutually beneficial relationship with the buyer and creativity on the specific matters that you would be working on. In general, firms spend too much time talking about their competency and comparative performance and too little talking about differentiation. Remember, too, that you can not only differentiate on the basis of service but on the basis of your ability to genuinely connect with the buyer during the presentation.

Adapting the Presentation to the Client's Learning Style

Just as you adapted your style in the needs-analysis interview to the personality type and learning style of the client representative, you should also adapt the style of your presentation. This is difficult, of course, if you will be presenting to several members of the client team. In that case, determine who the chief decision maker is and the personality type and information processing style of that individual, if possible, and let that learning style dominate your presentation. Is his or her style visual, auditory, or kinesthetic? In addition, during your dialogue with the various client representatives during the give-and-take of the presentation you can adapt to the style of each. But be careful not to lose the chief decision maker.

Here are the hallmarks of presentations in each of the three distinctive styles of processing information:

Visual: PowerPoint slides would seem to be the ideal medium for people who process information visually—but only if the slides are conceived correctly. As previously noted, slides that are merely text or script annoy visual

SOLUTIONS

processors. Does that mean then that you should produce slides with elaborate charts and graphs packed with information? Absolutely not. Remember, visual processors tend to be Sensers who like visuals that convey information quickly and succinctly. Use simple triangles, circles, and pyramids to get at the essence of the concepts you're presenting. And as you speak, paint word pictures when possible.

Auditory: With Auditory/Thinker types, who prefer evidence and reasoned analysis, you can use slides that provide the kinds of facts, figures, and evidence that are likely to sway this type of learner. With Auditory/Feeler types, who listen for values and sensitivity, the presentation should be a jumping off point for dialogue in which you can satisfy the Feeler's desire to connect with you. For this type of learner, don't load your slides with text in the mistaken belief that verbiage constitutes dialogue. Plan to genuinely engage the Auditory/Feeler in conversation. Dialogue can also be a powerful persuader with the Auditory/Thinker. Dialogue offers an opportunity for you to take this type of learner through an analysis with you, to reason together, and mutually arrive at clear, well-supported conclusions that he or she then owns.

Kinesthetic: The nature of presentations, with the listeners usually sedentary, works against connecting effectively with kinesthetic processors, whether they are Sensers who want to get to the point quickly or Intuitors who love big ideas. In many contexts, presenters can build in hands-on activities and frequent breaks that allow participants to move around as they talk. However, such devices can seem strained and hokey in a legal context. Again, as with Auditory types, the answer is dialogue. Kinesthetic processors tend to really come alive during discussion, especially if you toss them questions that give them an opportunity to express their feel for things. Also, don't be surprised if kinesthetics jump up during your discussion and start drawing on flip charts.

As these pointers suggest, simultaneously adapting your presentation to different personality/processing types is not as daunting as it might first seem. Through a judicious mix of the right kind of slides and, most importantly, agile and adaptable dialogue with each participant you can accomplish what at first might seem an impossibility: pleasing most of the people most of the time.

Delivering the Presentation

It should go without saying that before you deliver the presentation you should rehearse it—though beware of memorizing it to the point that it becomes robotic, with no room for spontaneity or give and take. Typically, three rehearsals are enough to give you some sense of how the presentation is going to unfold. Videotape all three and review the tape. And be sure to allow time in your presentation for dialogue and questions.

You should select the meeting site for the presentation, if you have the opportunity, and view the facilities early if possible. If you are using computer-assisted presentation software, make sure the technology is working correctly. Arrange the room to coincide with your message. For example, if you want to convey the idea that the relationship will be a partnership, do not put your client or potential client on one side of the table and yourself on the other as if it were an international arbitration conference.

Above all, remember:

Presentations are not performances; they can be used to create deeper dialogue.

You should regard presentations as an opportunity to conduct further dialogue with the client or prospect. This dialogue is a continuation of the needs assessment that you have done earlier. The presentation should verify that you will deliver what they are looking for, not that you have great stage presence.

All interactions before, during, and after presentations or proposal discussions create impressions. It is very difficult to recover if you've made a poor first impression. Be especially aware of the interplay among the members of your team. You will not get a second chance to overcome a bad first impression. To avoid creating bad impressions, remember to focus on the client's needs as opposed to what you want to sell. Focus also on the value of what you are offering, not simply on price. Your goal is to communicate how your services bring value to their business, i.e., increased profits or the protection of valuable assets.

In summary, use presentations or proposals to move your ideas through the client's organization in a way that gets them to take ownership of the ideas. Presentations are a way for you to *demonstrate* your expertise, your differentiation, your value-added solutions, and your willingness to engage the client or prospect in a genuine exchange of ideas that foreshadows the kind of working relationship you will create.

Following Up on the Presentation

Once you've completed your presentation you're left with the question: "Where do we go from here?" By all means, ask. There are a number of ways to phrase the process question:

- "Who else needs to look at this decision?"

- "What additional information might you need?"

- "In what timeframe do you see this decision being made?"

- "How are we doing so far?"

- "Where do we go from here?"

If you have demonstrated real understanding of their needs, persuasively established your ability to fill those needs, specified exceptional service, and created a real connection, then the client will likely proceed. However, sometimes no matter how good your solution may be, the timing for the client or prospect may simply be wrong. Resist the urge to pressure them:

 Any pressure you put on people who are not ready will cause them to retreat from you—maybe for all time.

If you fail to get a go-ahead, it could be based on any number of factors. It could be a mismatch in communication styles, lack of rapport and trust within your team that the client becomes aware of, or lack of trust between the team and the client or prospect. The decision process may not be entirely clear and you failed to ask the process question. Further, the client or prospect may not have viewed your solutions as having the requisite value they were seeking. They may not recognize their needs, and they may still have some unresolved concerns that have little to do with you or your firm. You may have also embarked on too aggressive selling as opposed to responding to their needs.

In any case, try to get the prospect or client to provide you with a candid explanation for deciding not to continue with you. You will not only gather information that can be useful for improving your performance but also demonstrate your continuing interest in the client—and leave the door open for the future.

> **Rule:** You cannot persuade clients or prospective clients to buy before they are ready.

Success Story: Winning Business with a Client-Focused Presentation

A Mid-Atlantic firm had an opportunity to present to a global healthcare technology leader through a client referral. In the past, the firm would go in and do just that: present. Their presentations would be all about them and contain nothing about the prospect or client. After training with the author of this Field Guide, the firm took the five-step business development process to heart and tested it on this new opportunity. They had little to lose by changing their approach—their prior win rate was poor.

The group of three lawyers took the time to sit with the firm's marketing and client services team and come up with an agenda and an approach on what to ask at the pre-interview. Following significant research, the questions were highly customized. Focusing sharply on the client, the group conducted the pre-interview and asked about the communication styles of decision makers, their strategic plans, and business goals. As a result, the team then worked together to come back to the company with a customized presentation that explained how the firm could help the client company accomplish their goals. Wowed by the performance, the chief decision-maker for the client said "You really understand our business." Within two weeks, they hired the firm and in just two years the healthcare company became a million-dollar client.

SOLUTIONS

The Client Development and
Relationship Management Process—*Decision*

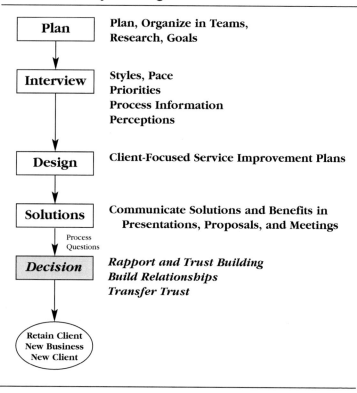

Plan	**Plan, Organize in Teams, Research, Goals**
Interview	**Styles, Pace** **Priorities** **Process Information** **Perceptions**
Design	**Client-Focused Service Improvement Plans**
Solutions	**Communicate Solutions and Benefits in Presentations, Proposals, and Meetings**
Process Questions	
Decision	*Rapport and Trust Building* *Build Relationships* *Transfer Trust*
Retain Client New Business New Client	

The Business Development Process: Decision

"It ain't over till it's over."

—Yogi Berra

During the previous stages of business development—Plan, Interview, Design, and Solutions—you have been building a relationship through interactions and conversations. Interestingly, the root of "conversation" is a Greek word meaning "convert." That is exactly what you have been trying to do: convert non-buyers to buyers through conversations designed to build trust.

Having heard you present your solutions, the client or prospect has several options: hire you, hire your competitor, delay the decision, do nothing, or do the work themselves. In this chapter you will learn what to do when you win the business and—more importantly—what to do if the client or prospect chooses one of the other options.

When You Win the Business

If the client or prospect promptly hires you, your next step is clear. Engage the client in a frank discussion about the deciding factors in your hiring. Was it your firm's reputation and experience? The value-added solutions? Your presentation? The trust you created? Cost? Then when you find yourself in similar business development situations you can be sure to replicate the things that worked.

DECISION

Also, find out what they didn't like. Press them to be as candid as possible. Make it clear that you don't take their criticism personally. If they are reluctant to criticize, assure them that it's important for you to know of any shortcomings that could potentially erode the relationship. Again, when you find yourself in similar business development situations in the future you can avoid those mistakes.

When the Client Chooses Another Option

When the client or prospect fails to hire you right away and pursues one of the other options, don't despair. Unless they have hired a competitor, which definitively forecloses the opportunity, the door may still be open. Don't burn your bridges, however. You never know when they might grow dissatisfied with their choice or face needs that you are uniquely qualified to fill. Further, even when you have lost to a competitor you can improve your performance in the future by asking the client or prospect why you weren't chosen.

In cases where the client or prospect has done nothing, delayed the decision, or decided to do the work in-house, you should also seek to understand why you weren't hired. You can start by reviewing all four previous stages of the business development process to see where you might have fallen short. For example, you may now realize that your planning failed to identify appropriate opportunities. Perhaps, during the interview stage, you failed to speak to enough people in the client organization and therefore produced an inadequate analysis of their needs. Maybe the design of your solution did not adequately explain how the relationship was going to work from a service standpoint. Or it could be simply that you misread the communication/learning style of the chief decision makers and failed to connect with them. In retrospect, these deficiencies may be quite clear to you.

However, such self-analysis goes only so far. You must also seek the candid assessment of the client or prospect. In the cases where the client has done nothing or delayed the decision, these conversations about your performance are doubly important. First, because as in the cases of the wins or outright losses these follow-up conversations will help you improve your performance in the future. Second, and most importantly in these cases, the follow-up conversations could well lead to converting these non-buyers into buyers. Remember:

 You may still have a chance of ultimately winning the business. Regard follow-up conversations as the continuation, not the end, of your business development effort with the client.

DECISION

You can initiate the follow-up conversations by returning to some of the process questions you asked in previous stages of the opportunity. For example, if they have done nothing or delayed the decision, you can ask, just as you did before you presented, where they are in the decision process. Ask whether they've completed their analysis and what factors might be holding them back from making a decision. Here is where you have the chance to pinpoint exactly the weaknesses in your performance—from inadequate planning to faulty needs analysis to an uncompelling presentation—and try to correct them, if the client or prospect is willing to let you do so.

You may discover that the chief obstacle standing in the way of a decision is something as simple as price. To use a medical analogy, the prospect may regard the proposed legal work as little more than treating a headache, while you regard it as brain surgery. In that case, you should try to understand where you may have failed to relate the value you are offering to the price you are asking and offer to make the case more clearly. Also, ask open-ended questions that might help change the prospect's perception of the value. For example, suppose you have proposed handling an IPO for a prospect's privately-held company for $500,000. The prospect tells you that she has been quoted $150,000 by another firm. You might then ask what the company expects for that $150,000, or what they will do if the IPO doesn't go through. Each situation is of course unique, but the key is to induce the client to explore further the real value you are offering.

In the course of a conversation about the stalled decision, you should offer to assist them in further understanding the risks of moving forward versus not moving forward. Ask as well who is involved in the decision at this point. If it is someone with whom you have not previously met, offer to make yourself available to answer questions and discuss your proposal. Offer also to repeat your presentation to this decision maker.

Although, as previously noted, you should avoid old-fashioned sales techniques, there may come a point in these follow-up conversations when it's perfectly appropriate to open directly the possibility of your being hired now. For example, if in a discussion of costs you have come up with innovative changes in your proposal that would address the client's concerns, you might say, "It appears to us that we do have a basis for moving forward with the relationship and what we would like to know here at our firm is how you see this moving forward?" Or, having addressed those cost concerns, you might simply say, "What are the next steps from your perspective?"

But make this move advisedly. Using consumer sales techniques that might work for a salesman in an appliance store to force people to buy are inappropriate here. Unlike the appliance salesman, you are not in a one-time sales situation; you are trying to build a relationship for the long term. Give the client or prospect room to buy and give them the sense that they are freely making the decision, not being pressured. Even if you don't win the business this time, there may be other opportunities with this client or prospect in the future—but not if you alienate them with high-pressure tactics.

Dealing With Rejection and Anxiety

One of the things that many lawyers struggle with at the decision stage is the emotional impact of rejection. But by asking the process questions, you move the conversation onto an objective, impersonal level where your ego is not at stake. Often you will discover in these conversations that the roadblocks to a favorable decision have little to do with you, whereas if you neglect to engage in these discussions you might walk away with a completely unwarranted sense of failure. You may also discover that what you regard as rejection is actually cause for mild celebration. For example, if the client or prospect says "We are not ready now," that signals that you have in fact developed the person into a potential buyer for the future.

DECISION

Much anxiety also attends the decision stage. One effective way to deal with that anxiety is to keep your pipeline full of opportunities. If an opportunity that has reached the decision stage is on hold or appears to be going nowhere, turn energetically to other opportunities and return to the stalled one later. To the client who is not ready, simply say, "When you are ready, please let us know," and try to get some sense of when they might be willing to revisit the decision.

With a full pipeline of opportunities at various stages of development, you won't feel the overwhelming—and often counterproductive—need to close the deal when you have only a few opportunities simmering. Our experience has been that somewhere between 50 to 100 opportunities that you are working on over a long period of time will not only provide you with a steady flow of business but also give you the luxury of choosing the most profitable business—the ultimate goal of business development.

A Final Word

You now have the tools for taking a step-by-step, proven approach to business development. Use them systematically and—far from having to ward off anxiety and suffer rejection—you will likely be celebrating more success than you thought possible. You can go forth confidently, secure in the knowledge that you will be genuinely serving client needs and creating the trust that is the foundation of long-term client relationships and the bedrock of a satisfying career.

> **Rule:** To build lasting trust with clients, trust the process and trust yourself.

Success Story: Converting a Loss into Victory

A large East Coast firm faced a beauty contest conducted by a major energy client for its workers' compensation work. Although the client remarked that the firm's team gave the best presentation, the client twice requested a reduction in price. Having researched and documented that the work would be unprofitable at the discounted price, the firm declined. The work went to a competitor who would be working for a commodity rate.

Despite this initial outcome, the firm gathered valuable information about the client's perception of the firm and formed a team specifically tasked with safeguarding existing work with the client. Subsequently, when a highly-placed, new in-house lawyer requested a meeting to review current litigation the firm's lawyers gathered from their contacts such intelligence as how to present, who would make decisions, and what was expected to result from the meeting. A menu of topics, based on feedback from the client, was prepared for the meeting. Lawyers met twice to rehearse and each time refined their message and delivery. As a result, the new in-house lawyer visibly gained respect for the litigators during the meeting. In addition, the firm brought along a specialist in an area where the lawyers knew the client needed coverage, and he wowed the clients with his expertise.

Following the client visit, the client interviewed three competitors for work in an area where the firm had been perceived to be weak. As a result of the prior meeting with the client, however, the firm had been able to change client perceptions and win an interview for the

DECISION

work. By persisting in understanding client needs, continuing to be guided by profitability, and refusing to give up, the firm had lost the commodity work, which it could not do profitably, but gained the more profitable work in an area where the firm was formerly perceived to be weak.

Appendix A: Business Development for Firms of Differing Sizes and Types

Solo Practitioners, Boutiques, and Small Firms

If you are a solo practitioner, boutique, or small firm, you need to spend as many waking hours as possible meeting with clients and prospective clients face-to-face conducting the needs analysis. From those needs analyses, you will be able to develop your niche and develop the specialty that will set you apart in experience and knowledge from your competition.

However, you must also understand their perception of where you are on the buyer's value curve (Figure 6, The Cobb Value Curve, developed by William C. Cobb in his article "How To Create Real Added Value," 2000). Are you considered to be a rare talent for whom people are willing to pay high rates or are you considered to be a lawyer who typically does commodity work? Does the buyer think that the proposed work is a commodity, while you think it's closer to a nuclear event? As discussed in the Decision chapter, you have to change the buyer's perception of the value of the work rather than simply cave in on price.

Figure 6. The Cobb Value Curve

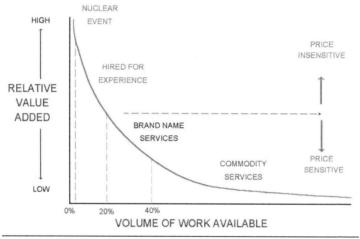

The Competitive Position Profile

© William C. Cobb of Cobb Consulting; Houston, Texas. Used with permission.

Unfortunately, in our experience, we have found that many lawyers, suffering from "economic low self-esteem," are all too willing to let themselves be beaten up on price. Moreover, in-house lawyers know that, and they know that many lawyers dislike business development. As a result, they are often able to run roughshod over outside counsel on the matter of price. But if you have fairly and accurately priced your services, there is no reason you should back down on price. Rather, make clear the value of what you are offering. And be prepared to walk away, if necessary. In the long run, standing behind the value of your services, rather than being ready to discount your price, will contribute far more to your long-term profitability.

Other actions you can take to increase the success of your business development efforts include:

Be willing to retool. If, for example, you are doing unprofitable litigation for clients, you may want to consider going to commercial clients where those trial skills would be more valued.

Spend time understanding your current clients and why they buy. Then carry what you learn into encounters with other prospective clients. Typically, likeability and client service rule in their world.

Build your network of referrals. Seek references from your current clients and permission to use them in seeking new business. Chances are if your current clients are not already recommending you to other people your solicitation of a reference will spur them to do so.

Develop stories both in written form and oral form that demonstrate the value that clients have received from you. Ideally, these case studies would reference those clients by name, but often the sensitive nature of the issues and the client's unwillingness to go public will require you to disguise the client's identity. (Of course, never use a client's name in marketing and business development materials without written permission.) Use the familiar problem-solution-benefits structure for these case studies. Succinctly state the client's problem in the first paragraph. Describe in the second paragraph your solution and its uniqueness. In the third paragraph, discuss the benefits that accrued to the client as a result of your solution.

Keep your pipeline full. Even if you find business development distasteful—and you shouldn't now that you have the tools—don't let your efforts flag. You don't want to look ahead 60 days and find that you have no prospects for business on the horizon.

Measure your return on investment. You need concrete proof that the actions you are taking are in fact yield-
ing results.

Midsize and Large Firms

Avoid operating your firm like a shopping mall—functioning
as a series of boutiques or small retail stores within a larger
shopping mall called the firm. You need to build cross-func-
tional, interdisciplinary teams. The shopping mall structure
works against the client-focused team approach to business
development with large, key clients—which should be your
most important effort.

As detailed in the Plan chapter, you will need to divide your
market into three distinct segments: 1) the large key clients
or your Top 150; 2) all the rest of your clients; and, 3) new
clients and referrals. Build teams around key clients rather
than practice groups. Each one of those segments will need
a discrete set of tactics. There's no one-size-fits-all approach,
especially with the key clients. Each key client needs a separate marketing and business development plan developed in
collaborative fashion by the team dedicated to that client.
The quality of business development results will depend on
the internal conversations within those teams focused on an
action plan to increase profit.

Of course you should also have practice group business development plans. And practice groups will need to be marketed within the firm to client teams that have a need. For
example, litigation practice groups should be formed and
marketed internally. New client marketing would use the
practice group plans to capture the client initially and then
later bring in the "Trojan horse" called the firm.

Use metrics to cull unprofitable clients. However, do it gradually. In most firms, typically 25 to 35 percent of the clients are unprofitable, regardless of their size. There are a number of software programs on the market that can help you calculate client profitability.

You should also devise a way to measure your business development actions. If you cannot measure the action, it is going to be difficult to manage; and if you cannot manage it, it is probably not something you should be doing.

Spending face-time with clients and prospective clients for some of the larger law firms is an advantage. The partners can spend upwards of 400 hours in business development. For smaller firms it is more difficult to spend that amount of time because you are trying to perform and bill the work. Nevertheless, solo practitioners, boutiques, small firms, mid-size firms, and large firms alike, need to be able to seek not just more work but more profitable work.

Corporate and Government Lawyers

Corporate and government entities also have clients. All of the principles in this book apply directly to building relationships with the users of their services. For example, the costs for legal services in some cases are charged back to the users, which may cause the individuals who have responsibility for those business units to actually see reductions in their paychecks.

Think carefully about the impact of legal services on the internal buyer. Perform the needs analysis, build the relationship, understand the service needs of your internal clients, understand their business, and develop approaches that enable you to ensure that the legal climate of the company or the government entity is free of legal landmines. For example, many legal problems often result from business people unwittingly making what are essentially legal decisions, often landing the organization in litigation or other problems. You can avoid these disasters-in-the-making by keeping your finger on the pulse of the business from a legal point of view and by making sure that non-legal people better understand the areas where legal counsel is advisable.

Appendix B: Opinion Surveys Can Help Keep Clients Happy

By William J. Flannery, Jr.

For a law firm to survive, it must serve its clients well. Yet most firms do not have an organized method to evaluate their clients' perceptions of the firm's performance. Without client feedback, the firm's management cannot determine the strength of the relationship.

The client opinion survey is one of the best ways to measure client satisfaction. A well-designed and properly conducted survey also can provide information that will help the firm make decisions on marketing, growth, fee determination, and practice emphasis.

Questions to be considered by a firm planning to conduct a client opinion survey include:

1. What is the survey's purpose?

The purpose will dictate the type of information to be collected. Most firms will find themselves in an endless debate trying to determine what each lawyer wants to see on the survey. A way to avoid that trap is to designate a small group of lawyers and the appropriate support staff to define the purpose and select the survey questions.

2. Who should be surveyed?

Business and institutional clients are accustomed to participating in customer-satisfaction surveys and probably would participate in written or face-to-face programs on an annual basis. The most important clients of the firm should be interviewed face-to-face in the client's office.

Certain types of consumer practices, personal injury, bankruptcy, and family law need to get feedback from clients immediately. These clients should be surveyed using comment cards after every office visit.

3. Who should conduct the survey?

This is another topic that can cause endless debate. The firm should delegate the management of the program to no more than three or four lawyers and the firm's marketing and business development professionals. Although many lawyers believe that the best people to conduct the survey are public relations agencies and consultants, an effective survey is one that gets to the bottom of the issues, and outsiders don't always know the proper follow-up questions to ask. Surveys also can be opportunities to market the firm's capabilities, and outsiders obviously cannot perform that function.

The most critical qualifications for the people conducting the survey are the abilities to communicate and to show empathy, trust, and concern for the client's well-being. The interviewers also should have some knowledge of the client's business and key decision makers and should have received training in listening skills and questioning techniques.

Most of the initial interviews will be face-to-face, and training in body language will be important. The training should include a pretest of the questionnaire, with the interviewers being videotaped conducting interviews with mock clients.

4. When should the survey be conducted?

Now. Client satisfaction is the best measure of a firm's stability and future. Firms that don't have a way to measure client satisfaction will eventually see the results of poor client relationships in less palatable ways than merely unpleasant answers to a survey.

The most obvious is when the client fires the firm. Often a client feels hurt because of the firm's perceived indifference and shifts its business away from the firm quietly and without the firm's knowledge.

This scenario often is accompanied by a panic attack by the firm or a "diplomatic mission" to determine why the firm is no longer getting its share of the client's legal business. If the firm has to ask for its "fair share," it probably is too late to save the relationship.

Although many firms are reluctant even to broach the subject of client surveys for fear of offending their partners, this reluctance needs to be overcome. Some partners may feel they are being pressured or scrutinized unfairly. The firm needs to help them realize that this is not the purpose of the survey. The firm also needs to recognize and accept that it may hear bad news from its clients.

Clients are not reluctant to give their opinions, and firms that ask the tough questions generally are viewed as caring and attentive. It is clear that the best way to determine client satisfaction is to ask the client.

Interview Blueprint

The interviewing techniques will be critical to the success of the relationship between the firm and the client and the quality of the information the firm receives. The questions should be open and allow for detailed feedback. The questioning style should avoid interrogating the client.

If the client should become offended or confrontational, the interviewer should employ reflective listening techniques to understand the true nature of the client's dissatisfaction.

The following areas should be discussed and tailored for each client interview:

1. an evaluation of the firm's performance on all matters;

2. performance evaluation of the specific practice areas used by the client;

3. performance evaluation of the partner responsible for the client;

4. performance evaluation of the other lawyers who have worked on the client's matters;

5. performance evaluation of the quality of service provided in document preparation, informational systems support, paraprofessional support, telephone and voice mail, electronic mail and facsimile communications, and administrative support;

6. quality of advice and counsel;

7. quality of the work product;

8. firm's recognition and fulfillment of client's needs;

9. clarity of the billing procedures and fee arrangements;

10. accessibility of the firm's partners and other key personnel;

11. whether the firm has kept the client informed;

12. the firm's strengths and weaknesses;

13. the firm's reputation within the community or industry;

14. areas for improvement;

15. competitive analysis—the firm compared to other firms or alternatives;

16. willingness to refer others to the firm;

17. value the client has received for its investment in the firm;

18. the client's view of the firm's approach to matters on which it has worked;

19. responsiveness of the individual lawyers and the firm to the client; and

20. how the firm has shown that it cares about the client.

Implementing a Survey

The basic steps from the time the firm decides that a client survey makes good sense until the completion of the survey are:

1. Select a management team.

2. Select clients to be surveyed.

3. Create the questions for the survey.

4. Select the interviewers.

5. Train the interviewers.

6. Conduct the survey.

7. Review the results and take action.

The missing link in these steps is what to do after you learn that you have a client dissatisfaction problem. That next step is to implement a client relationship management program. A more common name is client development. Some firms call client satisfaction programs by another name—marketing. The real challenge for most firms is to get started doing something other than talking about client satisfaction.

Clients often comment that lawyers need to pay more attention to the client's bottom line rather than their own. Client opinion surveys are unique tools for assessing the quality of the relationship with a client and at the same time determine how the client feels about the firm's contribution to the client's bottom line.

Without a client opinion survey, there is no ongoing, positive way for a firm to measure the success of its service strategy and its clients' perception of that strategy.

This article appeared in the June 11, 1990 issue of *Texas Lawyer.*

Appendix C: Gems and Rules

 How you think is everything.

 People can be trained to be better at business development, marketing, building trust, and managing profitable client relationships.

 Passion is a great motivator and can play a significant role in helping you become proactive about your clients' needs.

 Successful business developers seek to understand the clients' needs before they provide solutions. As Stephen R. Covey, the author of *The 7 Habits of Highly Effective People*, says, "Seek first to understand, then to be understood."

Rule: Persistence can turn "no" today into a "yes" tomorrow. Never give up.

 Focus strategy on the most profitable business.

 Let strategy drive the allocation, design, and content of marketing efforts.

 Design marketing activities to result in face-to-face business development opportunities.

> **Rule:** Strategy targets the most profitable business; marketing seeks to create face-to-face development opportunities for winning that business.

 The ultimate purpose of the planning process is to win a face-to-face meeting in which by having done your homework and listening carefully you can identify opportunities to meet the needs of existing clients and prospects.

 Find out as much as possible about the client contacts and the client's business.

> **Rule:** Use research to help design client needs-analysis questions.

 Better interpersonal communication can mean more opportunities to work.

 In adjusting your communication style, your goal is not mimicry, but to use learning methods and provide experiences that match people's preferences.

 With existing clients, interviewing for needs should take place continually and concurrently with the delivery of services.

> **Rule:** When interviewing, listen and don't pitch.

 Do not confuse designing the service plan with crafting the client presentation.

Distinguish between legal services, value-added services, and service quality.

Rule: Make the invisible—service—visible, tangible, and measurable.

 Involve the client or prospect as a coach on how you should present your solutions.

 Presentations are not performances; they can be used to create deeper dialogue.

 Any pressure you put on people who are not ready will cause them to retreat from you—maybe for all time.

Rule: You cannot persuade clients or prospective clients to buy before they are ready.

 You may still have a chance of ultimately winning the business. Regard follow-up conversations as the continuation, not the end, of your business development effort with the client.

Rule: To build lasting trust with clients, trust the process and trust yourself.

Bibliography

Plan

Alessandra, Anthony J., and Phillip L. Hunsaker. *The Art of Managing*. New York: Simon & Schuster, 1990.

Anderson, Rolph E., and Joseph F. Hair. *Professional Sales Management*. New York: McGraw Hill, 1988.

Beckwith, Harry. *The Invisible Touch: The Four Keys to Modern Marketing*. New York: Warner Books, 2000.

Bennis, Warren. *Why Leaders Can't Lead*. Los Angeles: Jossey-Bass Publishers, 1989.

Bennis, Warren, and Burt Nanus. *Leaders, The Strategies for Taking Charge*. New York: Harper & Row, 1985.

Biehl, Bob. *Increasing Your Leadership Confidence*. Sisters, OR: Questar Publishers, 1989.

Burrus, Daniel, with Roger Gittines. *Technotrends*. New York: HarperBusiness, 1993.

Collins, Jim. *Good to Great*. New York: HarperCollins Publishers, Inc., 2001.

Collins, James C., and Jerry I. Porras. *Built to Last*. New York: Harper Business Essentials, 2002.

Covey, Stephen R. *The 7 Habits of Highly Effective People*. New York: Simon & Schuster, 1990.

Covey, Stephen R. *Principle-Centered Leadership*. New York: Summit Books, 1990.

Cox, Jeff, and Eliyahu M. Goldratt. *The Goal*. Great Barrington, MA: North River Press, 1992.

Dobyns, Lloyd, and Clare Crawford-Mason. *Quality or Else*. Boston: Houghton Mifflin Company, 1991.

Donnellon, Anne. *Team Talk*. Boston: Harvard Business School Press, 1996.

Durham, James A., and Deborah McMurray, editors. *The Lawyer's Guide to Marketing Your Practice, Second Edition*. Chicago: American Bar Association, 2004.

Friedman, Lawrence, Neil Rackham, and Richard Ruff. *Getting Partnering Right*. New York: McGraw-Hill, Inc., 1996.

Goleman, Daniel. *Emotional Intelligence*. New York: Bantam Books, 1995.

Goleman, Daniel. *Working With Emotional Intelligence*. New York: Bantam Books, 1998.

Grella, Thomas C., and Michael L. Hudkins. *The Lawyer's Guide to Strategic Planning*. Chicago: American Bar Association, 2004.

Heiman, Stephen E., and Robert B. Miller. *Strategic Selling*. Berkeley, CA: Warner Books, 1987.

Heiman, Stephen E., and Robert B. Miller. *Successful Large Account Management*. New York: Henry Holt Co., 1991.

Hendricks, Gay, and Kate Ludeman. *The Corporate Mystic.* New York: Bantam Books, 1996.

Hessan, Diane, and Richard Whiteley. *Customer-Centered Growth*. Reading, MA: Addison-Wesley Publishing Company, 1996.

Hiebeler, Robert, Thomas B. Kelly, and Charles Ketteman. *Best Practices*. New York: Simon & Schuster, 1998.

Kanter, Rosabeth Moss. *The Change Masters*. New York: Touchstone Books, 1983.

Katzenbach, Jon R., and Douglas K. Smith. *The Wisdom of Teams*. Boston: Harvard Business School Press, 1993.

Kline, David, and Kevin G. Rivette. *Rembrandts in the Attic*. Boston: Harvard Business School Press, 2000.

Kotler, Philip. *Kotler on Marketing*. New York: The Free Press, 1999.

Kotter, John P. *Leading Change*. Boston: Harvard Business School Press, 1996.

Krass, Peter. *The Book of Leadership Wisdom*. New York: John Wiley & Sons, Inc., 1998.

Lencioni, Patrick. *The Five Dysfunctions of a Team: A Leadership Fable*. San Francisco: Jossey-Bass, 2002.

Madigan, Charles, and James O'Shea. *Dangerous Company*. New York: Times Business, 1997.

Maister, David H. *Managing The Professional Service Firm*. New York: The Free Press, 1993.

Maxwell, John C. *The 17 Indisputable Laws of Teamwork*. Nashville: Thomas Nelson Publishers, 2001.

Peters, Thomas J. *In Search of Excellence*. New York: Harper & Row, 1982.

Peters, Thomas J. *A Passion For Excellence*. New York: Random House, 1985.

Peters, Thomas J. *Thriving On Chaos*. New York: Knopf, 1987.

Pfeffer, Jeffrey, and Robert I. Sutton. *The Knowing-Doing Gap*. Boston: Harvard Business School Press, 2000.

Pfeffer, Jeffrey. *Managing With Power*. Boston: Harvard Business School Press, 1992.

Quick, Thomas L. *Successful Team Building*. New York: AMACOM, American Management Association, 1992.

Rackham, Neil. *Major Account Sales Strategy*. New York: McGraw Hill, 1989.

Rackham, Neil, and Richard Ruff. *Managing Major Sales*. New York: HarperBusiness, 1991.

Riskin, Gerald A. *Powerful Strategies for Transforming Your Practice*. Chicago: American Bar Association, 2005.

Sandhausen, Richard L. *Marketing*. New York: Barron, 1987.

Seligman, Martin E.P. *Learned Optimism*. New York: Alfred A. Knopf, Inc., 1990.

Senge, Peter M. *The Fifth Discipline*. New York: Doubleday, 1990.

Senge, Peter M. *The Fifth Discipline Fieldbook*. New York: Doubleday, 1994.

Sonnenberg, Frank K. *Marketing to Win*. New York: Harper & Row, 1990.

Tracy, Brian. *Advanced Selling Strategies*. New York: Fireside, 1995.

Treacy, Michael, and Fred Wiersema. *The Discipline of Market Leaders*. New York: Addison-Wesley Publishing, 1995.

Zeughauser, Peter D. *Lawyers Are From Mercury, Clients Are From Pluto*. Newport Beach, CA: ClientFocus, 1999.

Interview

Ailes, Roger. *You Are The Message*. New York: Doubleday, 1988.

Alessandra, Anthony J. *Non-Manipulative Selling*. New York: Wexler & Barrera, Prentice Hall Press, 1989.

Alessandra, Tony, and Michael J. O'Connor. *The Platinum Rule*. New York: Warner Books, Inc., 1998.

Beckwith, Harry. *Selling the Invisible*. New York: Warner Books, 1997.

Bolton, Robert. *People Skills*. New York: Simon & Schuster, 1979.

Boothman, Nicholas. *How to Make People Like You in 90 Seconds Or Less*. New York: Workman Publishing Company, Inc., 2000.

Bosworth, Michael T. *Solution Selling*, Burr Ridge, IL: Irwin Professional Publishing, 1995.

Brooks, Michael. *The Power of Business Rapport*. New York: Harper Collins Publishers, 1991.

Burley-Allen, Madelyn. *Listening: The Forgotten Skill*. New York: Wiley & Sons, 1982.

Cathcart, Jim. *Relationship Selling*. New York: Putnam Publishing Group, 1990.

Davis, Kevin. *Getting Into Your Customer's Head*. New York: Times Business, 1996.

Gray, John. *Men Are From Mars, Women Are From Venus*. New York: HarperCollins Publishers, Inc., 1992.

Gschwandtner, Gerhard. *Non Verbal Selling Power*. Englewood Cliffs, NJ: Prentice Hall, 1985.

Heiman, Stephen E., and Robert B. Miller. *Conceptual Selling*. Berkeley, CA: Warner Books, 1987.

Heller, Robert. *Communicate Clearly*. New York: DK Publishing, Inc., 1998.

Hopkins, Tom. *How to Master the Art of Selling*. New York: Warner Books, 1980.

Humes, James C. *The Ben Franklin Factor: Selling One to One*. New York: William Morrow & Company, Inc., 1992.

Lofland, Donald J., Ph.D. *Power Learning*. Stamford, CT: Longmeadow Press, 1992.

McDermott, Ian, and Joseph O'Connor. *NLP—First Directions*. London: Thorsons, HarperCollins Publishers, Inc., 2001.

Parinello, Anthony. *Selling to VITO: The Very Important Top Officer*. Holbrook, MA: Bob Adams, Inc., 1994.

Pease, Allan, and Barbara. *The Definitive Book of Body Language*. New York: Bantam Dell, 2006.

Peppers, Don, and Martha Rogers. *The One to One Future*. New York: Doubleday, 1993.

Peppers, Don, and Martha Rogers. *The One to One Enterprise*. New York: Doubleday, 1997.

Pertlta, Naomi W. *Talking & Listening*. Chicago: Institute of Financial Education, 1990.

Tannen, Deborah. *Talking From 9 To 5*. New York: William Morrow and Company, 1994.

Tannen, Deborah. *You Just Don't Understand*. New York: William Morrow and Company, 1990.

Walton, Donald. *Are You Communicating?* New York: McGraw Hill, 1989.

Design

Albrecht, Karl, and Ron Zemke. *Service America!* New York: Warner Books, 1985.

Davidow, William H., and Bro Uttal. *Total Customer Service: The Ultimate Weapon.* New York: Harper Perennial, 1989.

Gronroos, Christian. *Service Management and Marketing.* Lexington, MA: Lexington Books, 1990.

Hart, Christopher W.L., James L. Heskett, and W. Early Sasser, Jr. *Service Breakthroughs.* New York: The Free Press, 1990.

Nischwitz, Jeffrey L. *Think Again! Innovative Approaches to the Business of Law.* Chicago: American Bar Association, 2007.

Schaaf, Dick, and Ron Zemke. *The Service Edge.* New York: New American Library, 1989.

Whitely, Richard. *The Customer Driven Company.* Reading, MA: Addison-Wesley Publishing & The Forum Corp., 1991.

Zeithaml, Valarie A., Berry L. Leonard, and A. Parasuraman. *Delivering Quality Service.* New York: The Free Press, 1991.

Solutions

Buchan, Vivian. *Making Presentations With Confidence.* New York: Barron's Educational Series, Inc., 1991.

Jeary, Tony. *Life Is a Series of Presentations*. New York: Simon & Schuster, 2004.

Lambert, Clark. *The Business Presentations Workbook*. Englewood Cliffs, NJ: Prentice Hall, 1988.

Peoples, David A. *Presentations Plus*. New York: JohnWiley & Sons Inc., 1988.

Decision

Aubuchon, Norbert. *The Anatomy of Persuasion*. New York: AMACOM, 1997.

Bell, Arthur H., and Dayle M. Smith. *Winning with Difficult People*. New York: Barron's Educational Series, Inc., 1991.

Dawson, Roger. *Roger Dawson's Secrets of Power Negotiating*. Hawthorne, NJ: Career Press, 1995.

Fisher, Roger, and William Ury. *Getting to Yes*. New York: Penguin Group, 1981.

Hanan, Mack. *Consultative Selling*. New York: AMACOM, 1995.

Jandt, Fred E. *Win-Win Negotiating*. New York: John Wiley & Sons, 1985.

Jankowski, Mark A., and Ronald M. Shapiro. *The Power of Nice*. New York: John Wiley & Sons, Inc., 1998.

Loomis, Logan. *Both Sides Win! The 3 Secrets for Success in Customer Negotiations*. New Orleans: HBL Publishing, 2004.

McCormack, Mark H. *On Negotiating*. Beverly Hills, CA: Dove Books, 1985.

McKenna, Regis. *Relationship Marketing*. Reading, MA: Addison-Wesley Publishing Company, 1991.

Wallace, Kim, and Harry Washburn. *Why People Don't Buy Things*. New York: Perseus Books, 1999.

Extraordinary, Insightful Reading

Pink, Daniel H. A *Whole New Mind—Why Right-Brainers Will Rule the Future*. New York: Penguin Group, Inc., 2005.

Index

How to Start and Build a Law Practice, Platinum Fifth Edition

By Jay G Foonberg

This classic ABA bestseller has been used by tens of thousands of lawyers as the comprehensive guide to planning, launching, and growing a successful practice. It's packed with over 600 pages of guidance on identifying the right location, finding clients, setting fees, managing your office, maintaining an ethical and responsible practice, maximizing available resources, upholding your standards, and much more. If you're committed to starting—and growing—your own practice, this one book will give you the expert advice you need to make it succeed for years to come.

Making Partner: A Guide for Law Firm Associates, Second Edition

By John R. Sapp

Many factors come into play in achieving the goal of making partner: the quality of your work; how you relate to your superiors, fellow associates, and staff; how you entertain your clients; your choice of outside activities; even publications you read. It may take six to nine years, or more, to make partner from associate. Do you know what you should and should not be doing? Do you really know what your chances are at your firm? This concise, straightforward book looks at all these factors and provides detailed advice on how to create your own strategic plan for success. It's also the perfect primer to give to all new associates!

The Lawyer's Guide to Strategic Planning

By Thomas C. Grella and Michael L. Hudkins

This new resource is your guide to planning dynamic strategic plans and implementing them at your firm. You'll find specific suggestions on strategic planning for any size firm, in any practice area. You'll learn about the actual planning process and how to establish goals in key areas such as law firm governance, competition, financial management, technology, marketing and competitive intelligence, client development and retention, and much more. The book provides practical advice on how to implement your strategic plan at the tactical level, as well as how to monitor your progress so the firm remains on track with your vision. The accompanying CD-ROM also contains numerous policies, statements, and other sample documents you'll find indispensable in formulating your own process and plan.

Think Again! Innovative Approaches to the Business of Law

By Jeffrey L. Nischwitz

Think Again! is about creating a client-centric law firm and delivering great client service, differentiating your law firm from other firms, and developing the specific skills and strategies needed for effective and productive relationship building and business development results. You'll also learn the secrets of effective selling through existing relationships, how to take advantage of everyday opportunities, and consistent and reliable ways to bring new clients into the firm. It is no longer good enough to just be a good lawyer . . . lawyers need to be great managers, great client-service providers, great communicators, and great marketers. Rethink the way you do business, reposition your firm to stand out among your competitors, and reap the many benefits loyal and satisfied clients bring.